Sonata Form Innovations in Prokofiev's Nine Piano Sonatas

普羅高菲夫鋼琴奏鳴曲中

奏鳴曲式的傳承與創新 (英文版)

蔡佳憓 著

TSAI, CHIA-HUI

Sonata Form Innovations in Prokofiev's Nine Piano Sonatas

作　　者　蔡佳憓

出 版 者　蔡佳憓

美術顧問　蔡英謀

封面設計　陳宛君

出版日期　西元 2020 年 6 月 20 日

定　　價　新台幣 330 元

ISBN　978-957-43-7640-7

致中文版讀者

從聽覺美學而言，曲式可以說是一種深層的結構，提供辨識音樂歷程的進行軌跡；而奏鳴曲式之可塑性，提供了作曲家作實驗或大展身手的極佳平台。僅就表現奏鳴曲當中主題與副題，主調與副調之對比與統合，段落的轉折點，終止式的處理等等，其方法就變化多端。

本書邀請讀者一起來探索，普羅高菲夫是如何在這些使用奏鳴曲式和其變化型的樂章中，用極創新的方法，清楚地呈現出這些結構關鍵點 (structural points)。分析過程中所採用的部分術語，援用自詹姆斯・赫波柯斯基 (James Hepokoski) 和沃倫・達西 (Warren Darcy) 所提出的奏鳴曲式理論；分析和聲時所使用之和弦級數則直接以羅馬數字表示，並於中文版第二章之 (2) 為中文讀者補充重要術語說明。

由於中英文各有語法邏輯上的特點，當讀者在參考中譯本時 (全音出版)，會發現少數段落之陳述方式和文句順序並不會完全相同，建議讀者對照完整樂譜來理解。本書並不涉及主觀詮釋及演奏實務之探討，鼓勵讀者依據自己的興趣延伸閱讀，當對於樂曲理路有更清晰的理解時，持續按著「正道」練習，好作品自然會為自己發聲！

蔡佳憓

{ TABLE OF CONTENTS }

PREFACE

The nine piano sonatas by Serge Prokofiev comprise one of the towering productions in twentieth-century piano literature. They span the years from 1907 to 1947, a significant portion of his creative life. The first sonata, Op. 1, was begun during the time when Prokofiev was studying at the St. Petersburg Conservatory; the ninth, Op. 103, was the last work for solo piano, completed six years before his death in 1953. The sonatas provide an overview of Prokofiev's stylistic development, which encompasses romantic tendencies in the early time, the establishment of his original style, and the reflection of his later years as a Soviet citizen. One of the most striking features in these sonatas is his strictly designed classical form. All first movements are constructed in sonata-allegro form; four finales of the seven multi-movement sonatas are in sonata-rondo form. All second movements are in ternary form, which are followed either by ternary or rondo variants, with one exception in No. 2 that is repeated binary and one in No. 7, an arch form (See Table 1). This book will present how Prokofiev provides clear structural points in innovative ways within the sonata-allegro movements and those in sonata variants with analytical terminology derived from the sonata-form theory by James Hepokoski and Warren Darcy.

Table 1

	I	II	III	IV
No. 1	Sonata-allegro			
No. 2	Sonata-allegro	Ternary	Repeated binary	Sonata-allegro
No. 3	Sonata-allegro			
No. 4	Sonata-allegro	Ternary	Sonata-rondo	
No. 5	Sonata-allegro	Ternary	Sonata-rondo	
No. 6	Sonata-allegro	Ternary	Ternary	Sonata-rondo
No. 7	Sonata-allegro	Ternary	Arch form	
No. 8	Sonata-allegro	Ternary	Rondo	
No. 9	Sonata-allegro	Ternary	Rondo	Sonata-rondo

1

Introduction

(1) Biographical sketch

Serge Prokofiev was born on April 23, 1891, into a middle-class family in the village of Sontsovska in the Ukraine. He wrote his first piano piece at the age of five under his mother's guidance. In the spring of 1904, Prokofiev was brought by his mother to St. Petersburg. On the advice of Alexander Glazunov, then a faculty member at the St. Petersburg Conservatory who would become the director in 1905, Prokofiev applied for entrance. During the ten years of residence there, Prokofiev studied harmony and counterpoint with Anatole Liadov, orchestration with Nicolai Rimsky-Korsakov, conducting with Nicholas Tcherepnin, and piano with Alexander Winkler and Annette Essipova.

In 1914, Prokofiev visited London and met Igor Stravinsky and Serge Diaghilev, and saw their *Nightingale, Firebird, Petrushka,* and *The Rite of Spring*, as well as Maurice Ravel's *Daphnis and Chloe.* In 1917 before leaving Russia for a prolonged stay in the west to avoid the aftermath of the revolution, he completed piano sonatas Nos. 1 through 4. Prokofiev spent the years between 1918 and 1935, the so-called foreign period, mostly in the United States and France. In the piano works of this foreign period, Prokofiev absorbed the neo-classical aesthetics, which shares ideas similar to Stravinsky's aesthetics of emotional coolness and objectivity.[1] Piano Sonata No. 5 was completed during this period in 1923.

The Soviet period starts with Prokofiev's return to Russia in 1936; the last four sonatas were completed between 1939 and 1947. Prokofiev chose to remain in the Soviet Union for the rest of his life. With the outbreak of World War II, he possibly found the stimulus to react to the required patriotisms in the piano sonatas Nos. 6-8, and more explicitly in his opera *War and Peace* derived from Tolstoy's novel. Although he enjoyed many years of popularity in his homeland, as a Soviet composer he had to live with the

[1] David L. Kinsey, "The piano sonatas of Serge Prokofieff, a critical study of the elements of their styles" (Ph.D. dissertation, Columbia University, 1959), 296-297.

constant threat of bureaucratic condemnation. In later years, he had to endure the disappearance of his close associate, the theatrical director Vsevolod Meyerhold, periodic denunciation of his own music, and the sentencing of his first wife to eight years in a Siberian labor camp.[2] Prokofiev died on March 5, 1953, the same day that Stalin died.

(2) General styles in Prokofiev's nine piano sonatas

It was characteristic of Beethoven to "juxtapose the most original and the most conventional music ideas," and "exploit the conventional to create both a dramatic contrast and a splendid touch of irony."[3] Alongside those harmonic digressions and dramatic tonal shifts, the sonata hierarchy is never sacrificed for the sake of originality. Traditional harmonic functions always play a crucial part at every structural point, which provides a satisfactory audible resolution. More than a century after Beethoven's gigantic thirty-two piano sonatas, Prokofiev's nine sonatas provide another model for combining tradition and originality. In them, the temporary absence of conventional harmonic progression produces dramatic conflict: "this intricate web of connections, which may sustain itself over hours, while creating the irresistible impression of a unified argument and a comprehensive order, is achieved in the very surface that we hear."[4]

Prokofiev once summarized the essential elements in his music:

"The first was the classical line, which could be traced back to my early childhood and the Beethoven sonatas I heard my mother play…The second line, the modern trend, begins with that meeting with Taneyev when he reproached me for the "crudeness" of my harmony. At first this took the form of a search for my own harmonic language, developing later into a search for a language in which to express powerful emotion…Although this line covers harmonic language mainly, it also includes new departures in melody, orchestration and drama. The third line is the toccata, or the "motor" line traceable perhaps to Schumann's Toccata which made such a powerful impression on me when I first heard it…This line is perhaps the least important. The

[2] See Stephen C.E. Fiess, *The Piano Works of Serge Prokofiev* (New Jersey: The Scarecrow Press, 1994), 74.
[3] Charles Rosen, *Beethoven's Piano Sonatas: a Short Companion* (New Haven: Yale University Press, 2002), 173.
[4] Roger Scruton, *The Aesthetics of Music* (New York: Oxford University Press, 1999), 337.

fourth line is lyrical; it appears first as a thoughtful and meditative mood, not always associated with the melody, or, at any rate, with the long melody...This line was not noticed until much later...I should like to limit myself to these four "lines" and to regard the fifth, "grotesque" line which some wish to ascribe to me, as simply a deviation from the other lines. In any case I strenuously object to the very word "grotesque" which has become hackneyed to the point of nausea. As a matter of fact the use of the French word "grotesque" in this sense is a distortion of the meaning. I would prefer my music to be ascribed as "Scherzo-ish" in quality, or else by three words describing the various degrees of the word "Scherzo"—whimsical, laughter, mockery."[5]

The first four sonatas, which were composed before Prokofiev left Russia in 1918, are all in minor keys, undoubtedly because the minor mode gave more chances for the chromatic alternation that is one of the essential factors in his early music. The last five are in major keys. He created new effects in harmony and melody but did not experiment with form in his sonatas, for he believed the established form sufficient.[6]

P. R. Ashley has categorized Prokofiev's treatments of departure from traditional harmonic idioms into several types; Ashley's categories are summarized by Stephen C.E. Fiess in his "*The Piano Works of Serge Prokofiev*":

1) Harmonic side-slipping and substitution
2) Creation of new chords by oblique chromatic motion of one or more lines against a pedal point
3) Harmonic elision
4) Parallelism
5) Harmonies based on unusual scales
6) Unexpected modulations to foreign keys and unusual key relationships
7) Chromatic harmony
8) Polychords and superimposed chords

[5] S. Shlifstein, ed., *S. Prokofiev, Autobiography, Articles, Reminiscences*, trans. Rose Prokofieva (Moscow: Foreign Language Publishing House) 7, quoted in Rebecca G. Martin, "The nine piano sonatas of Sergei Prokofiev" (D.M.A. thesis, University of Kentucky, 1982) 4-5.
[6] Kinsey, 238.

9) Creation of new chords through added tones.[7]

Harmonic side-slipping is one way of substituting that uses neighbor chords in place of traditional chords, which sometimes results in a brief transition to a distant key. For instance, Prokofiev used harmonic side-slipping and substitution between two statements of the primary theme at the beginning of No. 6 to create a temporary tonal ambiguity in mm. 5-6, which also presents an example of superimposed chords. Other examples can be found in the first movements of No. 3 (mm. 22-25), No. 5 (mm. 14-15), No. 7 (mm. 124-143), No. 8 (mm. 35-41), and No. 9 (mm. 63-69). Chords generated by oblique chromatic motion of one or more lines against a pedal point can be found in No. 3 (mm. 123-131) and No. 5 (mm. 167-169).

Harmonic elision "refers to a compositional technique in which a chord normally present within a standard progression is omitted entirely or merely alluded to in passing." [8] Measure 19 in the first movement of No. 2 presents a clear example, in which the $\mathbf{V_7/v}$ is followed by i in D minor. This passage also contains chords with added notes to create a conflicting effect. The parallelism is applied in various ways that often scatter between sections such as mm. 95-97 in the first movement of No. 2; or support a melodic line such as mm. 132-140 in No. 3. Prokofiev utilized chromaticism both vertically and horizontally in the fast passage in the first movement of No. 8 (mm. 261-271). The innovative treatments disturb the unfolding of the expected deep structure. However, the structural points from most of the sonata movements are noticeably established (See Table 2). In the sonata-rondo movements, Prokofiev tended to use third relationships for tonal deployment more frequently. As in those sonata-allegro movements, Prokofiev's departure from convention is revealed through harmonic side-slipping (mm. 6-8 in the third movement of No. 4), chromatic harmony (mm. 17-18 in the third movement of No. 5), oblique chromatic motion (mm. 19-21 in the third movement of No. 5), and superimposed chords (mm. 97-112 in the fourth movement of No. 2). The overall tonal schemes are well defined despite those temporary harmonic excursions (See Table 2 and 3).

---

[7] Fiess, 15.
[8] Ibid., 18.

Table 2 : Tonal Deployment in Sonata Movements

	Exposition P theme	S theme	Development	Recapitulation (Except in No.7) P theme	S theme
No.1	Fm (i)	A^bM (III)	Modulatory fragmentation	Fm (i)	D^bM (IV) - Fm (i)
No.2 I IV	Dm (i) Dm (i)	Em (ii) CM (VII)	"	Dm (i) Dm (i)	Dm (i) Dm (i)
No.3	Am (i)	CM (III)	"	Am (i)	Am (i)
No.4 I	Cm (i)	E^bM (III)	"	Cm (i)	CM (I)- Cm (i)
No.5 I	CM (I)	Am (vi)	"	CM (I)	CM (I)
No.6 I	AM (I)	CM (III)- Am (i)	"	AM (I)	Am (i)-AM
No.7 I	B^b center	A^b center[9]	"	B^b center appear after S	B^b center
No.8 I	B^bM (I)	Gm (vi)- GM (VI)	"	B^bM (I)	B^bm (i)- B^bM (I)
No.9 I	CM (I)	GM (V)	"	BM (VII)	CM (I)

[9] One of the most noticeable ways to recognize structural points is the tonal deployment. Prokofiev sometimes used unusual tonal relationship between P and S themes, but eventually resolved the change and confirmed the tonic in the recapitulation. Examples can be found in the first movements of Nos. 2, 6, and 7, as well as the final movements of Nos. 2, 4, and 6.

Table 3 : Tonal Deployment in Sonata-rondo Movements

	Exposition P.	S.	Development P - New material	Recapitulation P. (Except in No. 5, 6)[10]	S.	Coda P.
	A	B	A - C	A	B	A
No.4 III	CM (I)	GM (V)	CM (I)- E^bM (^{b}III)	CM (I)	CM (I)	CM (I)
No.5 III	CM (I)	S: Modulatory passages over C	CM - P&S fragments in various modes	P2: Non-tonic key	CM (I)	P1 (I)
No.6 IV	Am (i)	S1: CM (III) – S2: over E-pedal (V)- S3: $G^\#m$($^\#$viim)	Am - Modulatory passages from Am based on P in first mvt.	P-based Modulatory passages from $F^\#m$ ($^\#$viim)	S3: Am -S2: over C pedal- S1:AM	P: Am
No.9 IV	CM (I)	GM (V)	CM (I) – E^bM (^{b}III)	CM (I)	CM (I)	Based on P CM (I)

[10] The third return of P in a sonata-rondo serves a recapitulating function by confirming the tonic or sometimes restating the complete P in a key other than the tonic. In the last movement of No. 5, and more obviously, in that of No. 6, the third-rotation P is not only stated in a key other than the tonic that interrupts the customary expectation for tonal resolution, but is also manipulated with developmental gesture and blended with episodic interpolations. Structurally speaking, this episodic P belongs to the development. The tonic is not stabilized until the reemergence of S, which recapitulates the S in the exposition back to the tonic.

2

Analytical concepts derived from sonata theory by James Hepokoski and Warren Darcy

From the aesthetic aspect, form can be understood as a pattern of "deep structure."[11] We can easily recognize the unfolding of deep structure in tonal music. Sonata form, for instance, provides the most flexible structure, since we can still recognize its "generative syntax" [12] within extended deformation. The polarity and centrality of the tonal organization in sonata form can be revealed in various ways. "Sonata form was an ordered system of generally available options permitting the spanning of ever larger expanses of time."[13] An analysis of major structural breaks "leads one into the heart of a productive, defensible sonata-form theory; the varying degree of rhetorical articulation—especially hierarchically ordered cadences, pauses, and breaks—are central to the mid- and late-eighteenth-century sense of form."[14] Hepokoski and Darcy, in their analysis of extensive instrumental works in the eighteenth century, find what they term "*interrelated family*."[15] They acknowledge this relatedness of family resemblances by "housing them all under the idea of differing sonata types."[16]

> "This is because all of the types share obviously similar structural principles. These include: a characteristic procedure of establishing an expositional layout consisting of functionally differentiated modules; a structure-determining dialogue with the principle of large-scale rotation; and the need for some sort of quasi-symmetrical tonal resolution in the last rotation of sonata-space. From this perspective, sonata-related structures may be usefully classified as being partitioned into **five broad categories or five different types**."[17]

In Hepokoski and Darcy's sonata theory, a usual exposition that has both primary and secondary themes includes the following structural sections or points: the ***primary-***

[11] Scruton, 310.
[12] Ibid.
[13] James Hepokoski and Warren Darcy, "The medial caesura and its role in the eighteenth-century sonata expositions" *Music Theory Spectrum: The Journal of the Society for Music Theory* 19 (Fall 1997), 153.
[14] Ibid., 115.
[15] James Hepokoski and Warren Darcy, "Elements of Sonata Form: the Late-Eighteenth-Century Sonata: Norms, Types, and Deformations." (Oberlin College Conservatory and Yale University, 1999, photocopy), 265.
[16] Ibid., 266.
[17] Ibid.

theme zone (**P**) that establishes the tonic, the ***medial caesura*** (**MC**) that is a structural punctuation built mostly around a strong half cadence to mark the end of the P zone and make possible the S zone, the ***secondary-theme zone*** in contrasting key (**S**), which remains until **EEC**, the ***essential expositional closure*** that bears the concluding cadential point in the exposition. The ***closing zone*** (**C**) may appear to reinforce the EEC. The ***transitional zone*** (**TR**) is often required to supply the energy toward the MC.[18] The TR is not necessarily modulatory. The structural zones or points in the exposition reappear in the recapitulation with **ESC**, the ***essential sonata closure***, as the corresponding part of the EEC in the exposition. The ***re-transitional zone*** (**RT**) is sometimes required to connect back to P zone or the tonic key.

Worth mentioning is that the MC can be achieved around an authentic cadence of secondary key, or less frequently, an authentic cadence of primary key, instead of a half cadence to the secondary key.

Among the five types of sonata form[19], type II, III, and IV formats can be found in Prokofiev's nine sonatas. Type III sonatas are the standard structure that includes exposition, development, and recapitulation that begins with the P theme typically in tonic. Its formal diagram can be demonstrated as followed in terms of Hepokoski and Darcy's sonata-form theory:

P—TR—MC—S—EEC—C—Development or Episode—RT—P—TR—MC—S—ESC—C—Coda

Type II sonatas offer a more complex range of varieties. The second appearance of P (Hepokoski and Darcy refer to it as second rotation), usually at the beginning of the recapitulation in other types, is treated in various ways. The second-rotation P is stated in keys other than the tonic, which interrupts the customary expectation for tonal resolution. It is often manipulated or blended in developmental expansions, interpolations, episodic substitutes, and the like. Structurally speaking, the second-rotation P belongs to the region of the development. The tonic is usually not stabilized until the reemergence of S, which recapitulates the S in the exposition back to the tonic. Thus the type II pattern

---

[18] Hepokoski and Darcy, *The medial caesura,*121.

[19] Type I is referred to as a sonata without development. Type V combines ritornello formats and procedures from eighteenth-century concerto movements.

sometimes gives the illusion of the "reversed-recapitulation"[20] effect. The type II pattern is not noticeable until one goes on to the materials after the exposition:

Exposition :

P-TR-MC-S-EEC-C

Development :

P (in non-tonic keys or substituted by other episodes)**-TR-MC**

Tonal resolution : (The term **"recapitulation"** is not used for type II.)

S-ESC-C

Coda :

P (If this section is provided, it often begins with sounding of P.)

The following diagram with roman numerals is derived from Hepokoski and Darcy's essay:[21]

The Type II Sonata (one typical pattern). Note: internal repeats of each rotations are optional; some Type IIs ask for both rotations to be repeated, while others not.

Rotation 1	**Rotation 2**		**(Not-Sonata-Space)**
Exposition	**Development**	**Tonal Resolution**	**(Coda [optional])**
P-TR-MC-S-EEC-C	**P-TR- MC**	**S- ESC- C**	
I V V	**V modulatory (Episodic substitutions for P are possible.)**	**I I**	**I (If this section is provided, it often begins with sounding of P.)**

[20] Hepokoski and Darcy, *Elements of Sonata Form*, 292.
[21] Ibid., 283.

Type IV sonatas include mainly a variety of sonata-rondo mixture. Some essential features are indispensable. In Hepokoski and Darcy's view:

> A piece or movement should not qualify as a true (full-scale) sonata-rondo, or Type IV sonata, unless its structure meet certain characteristics: First rotation is structured as the exposition of a sonata (**P TR MC S C**), and a later rotation recapitulates this expositional pattern. In other words, if the material following the refrain is structured as a simple period or hybrid in a contrasting key, the piece is probably a rondeau; if it is structured as a more elaborate binary form, the piece is a rondo; but if it is structured as a transition leading to a medial caesura followed by a secondary-theme zone (and perhaps a closing zone), and if this pattern is later recapitulated in the tonic key, then the sonata aspects of the piece are sufficiently strong that it should be considered a genuine sonata-rondo, or type IV sonata. . . . In dealing with type IV sonata, it is more accurate, more productive, to use the terminology of the sonata, not the rondo. [22]

Type IV sonatas usually combine the rondo rules with either type I without development in five-part rondo or type III in seven-part rondo. The comparison of a seven-part rondo and type IV sonata combined with type III features, in other words, the "type III sonata-rondo mixture" [23] can be illustrated as follows:

<table>
<tr><td colspan="7">Rondo :</td></tr>
<tr><td>A1</td><td>B</td><td>A2</td><td>C</td><td>A3</td><td>B</td><td>A4</td></tr>
<tr><td colspan="7">Type III Sonata-rondo Mixture :</td></tr>
<tr><td colspan="2">Exposition</td><td colspan="2">Development</td><td colspan="2">Recapitulation</td><td>Coda</td></tr>
<tr><td colspan="2">P TR-MC-S-EEC-C</td><td colspan="2">P New material or Episodes</td><td colspan="2">P TR-MC-S-ESC</td><td>P</td></tr>
</table>

Both type II and type IV have development initiated with P material that deceptively suggests either the recapitulation or the closing section of the exposition, while the exposition remains intact over the standard scheme. These terminologies serve as a reference to understand the deep structure in the sonata scheme manipulated by Prokofiev. Although the straightforward structural punctuations in eighteenth-century masterpieces can hardly be verified literally in Prokofiev's sonatas, one can still find the underlying correspondence disguised by his innovations, such as the methods of harmonic digression and others categorized by Ashley. In Prokofiev's writing, the MC, EEC, and ESC are not

---

22 Ibid., 338.

23 Ibid.

necessarily formed in obviously functional ways such as the V-I progression. I will examine all sonata-allegro and sonata-rondo movements of Prokofiev's piano sonatas with musical examples to support my analysis, which includes two principal issues: the underlying conventional structures of sonata movements and their variants in terms of concepts derived from Hepokoski and Darcy's sonata theory; and the harmonic as well as structural departures from sonata-form convention through Prokofiev's innovative composing manners taking Ashley's categorization as reference. Both issues are illustrated with detailed formal diagrams and musical examples.

3

Sonata No.1 in F minor, Op.1 (1909)

Around 1907-1908 Prokofiev composed six youthful piano sonatas, later referred to as "From Old Notebooks", during the time he was studying at the St. Petersburg Conservatory. Only the second, third, and fifth youthful sonatas in the "From Old Notebooks" were preserved in some way to be numbered sonatas in later stages. Sonata no. 1 was derived from the first movement of the youthful three-movement second sonata written in 1907. According to Israel Nestyev, Prokofiev's biographer in the Soviet Union, "Hackneyed figuration, pathetic minor themes in the spirit of Rachmaninoff and Medtner, touches reminiscent of Schumann . . . clearly dominated in this sonata over the few flashes of Prokofiev's own personality."[24]

No. 1 (*Allegro*) is a single-movement sonata. The harmony is for the most part functional; the triads are spiced with frequent emergences of eleventh and thirteenth chords. His fascination with the augmented-sixth chord is already noticeable in this piece.[25]

The structural deployment in terms of Hepokoski and Darcy's sonata theory is as followes: (Departures from conventional tonal scheme or Prokofiev's innovative treatments are shown in bold and italic)

Sonata No.1 in F minor Op.1 : Sonata-allegro (Type III)

STRUCTURE	MEASURE NUMBER	TONAL SHIFT
Introduction	1 – 4	Fm
Exposition		
P1	5 – 10	Fm
P2	11 – 15	Fm

[24] Israel V. Nestyev, *Sergei Prokofiev*, trans. by Rose Prokofieva (New York: Alfred A. Knopf, 1946), 20.
[25] See Patricia R. Ashley, "Prokofiev's Piano Music" (Ph.D. dissertation, Eastman School of Music, 1963), 15.

P1'	16 – 25	Fm
TR	25 – 41	Fm–B^{b}m–D^{b}M–A^{b}M
MC	41	$E^{b}{}_{7}$–(A^{b}M)
S1	42 – 57	A^{b}M
S1'	58 – 73	A^{b}M–D^{b}M–B^{b}m–E^{b}M–A^{b}M
S2	74 – 81	A^{b}M
S3	82 – 93	Fm–$E^{b}{}_{7}$–A^{b}M
EEC	92 – 93	$E^{b}{}_{7}$–A^{b}M
C	82 – 93	Fm–$E^{b}{}_{7}$–A^{b}M
<u>Development</u>		
C material	94 – 103	Fm–B^{b}m
TR material	104 – 115	B^{b}m–Dm–FM–Bm–$D^{\#}$m–$C^{\#}{}_{07}$
P & S fragments	116 – 133	Modulatory passages from GM to Fm with ***parallelism***
P as climax	134 – 145	Ends on C_7
<u>Recapitulation</u>		
P2 ***(P1 omitted)***	146 – 151	Fm–G_7
TR	152 – 173	Cm–Fm–B^{b}m–Em–GM–B^{b}m–$A^{b}{}_{7}$
MC	173	***$A^{b}{}_{7}$–(D^{b}M)***
S1	174 – 193	***D^{b}M***–Fm–C_7
S2	194 – 209	Fm
S3	210 – 218	Fm

ESC	217 – 218	Fm
S2	218 – 226	***Fm***
C	226 – 239	***Fm***
Coda	240 – 244	Fm

This analytical chart illustrates the tonal plan of No. 1 showing that of the nine sonatas it is the closest to convention. The F-minor tonic is introduced by the opening progression of Gr.$^{+6}$ and the dominant in F minor. The TR achieves its energy-gaining effect from F minor through continuous triplet motion to the cross-rhythm gesture emphasizing the $E^{b}{}_{7}$ chord that establishes a powerful MC before the onset of S in m. 42 (See Ex. 1-1).

【Ex. 1-1】 Prokofiev Sonata No. 1, mm. 37-42

The structural punctuation is somehow overlapped in m. 42. The downbeat on A^b brings TR to MC and meanwhile initiates the S zone without any caesura or dynamic dropout as in a traditional sonata. The exposition is closed with an authentic cadence in A^b major in m. 93, which seems to be an obvious EEC—the *essential expositional*

closure. However, the S2 passage in mm. 74-81 provides a musical gesture that strongly suggests a structural punctuation on the A^{b} downbeat in m. 82. The expectation of EEC in m. 82 is not sufficiently fulfilled by the following *closing zone* (C), which delays the real EEC effect and reinforces it through the *ff* arrival in mm. 92-93 (See Ex. 1-2 and Ex. 1-3).

【Ex. 1-2】 Prokofiev Sonata No. 1, mm. 73-84

【Ex. 1-3】 Prokofiev Sonata No. 1, mm. 91-94

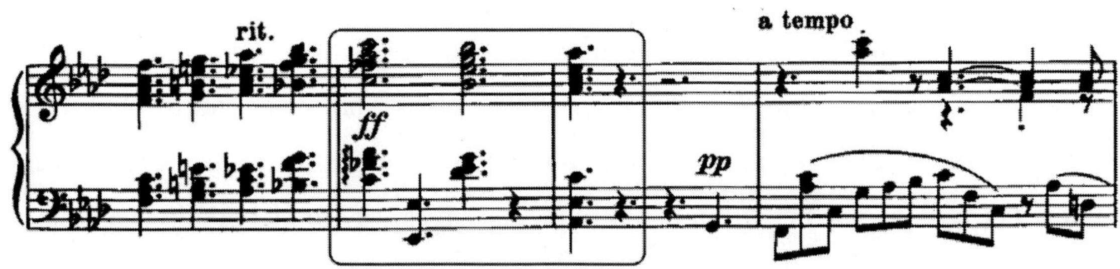

The recapitulation begins with P2. Prokofiev first made obscure and then reinforced the ESC in the same manner as in EEC, but inserted an S2 passage between the two sections based on S3 material, the latter one as *closing zone.* The last cadence is strongly implied on the empty downbeat at the beginning of the coda in m. 240 but actually delayed until the very last measure (See Ex. 1-4).

【Ex. 1-4】 Prokofiev Sonata No. 1, mm. 235-244

Oblique chromatic motion is the predominant method Prokofiev used to give temporary harmonic digression. The S1' section in mm. 58-73 goes from A^b major

through oblique chromatic motion to B^b minor and returns to A^b major. The passage of P and S fragments in mm. 116-133 of the development presents a modulatory passage from G major to F minor. P2 opens the recapitulation without the corresponding part of the antecedent P1 section. Harmonic side-slipping, chromatic harmony and parallel motion from F minor to G_7 occupy mm. 146-151 in the P2 section that leads to TR starting in C minor. The striking Gr.$^{+6}$ chord in the introduction gives way to diatonic iv^7 chords in the succinct coda. The final cadence is colored with a Fr.$^{+6}$ chord, which functions as a tritone substitute for the dominant (See Ex. 1-4).

The first piano sonata demonstrates noticeable structural points with harmonic gesture strongly suggesting the expected arrivals. Although later sonatas depart further from the conventional design harmonically, these structural punctuations never fail to find their place in the generative process.

4

Sonata No.2 in D minor, Op.14 (1912)

Sonata No. 2 was completed in 1912 during Prokofiev's stay in the warm and bright mountain resort of Kislovodsk.[26] The second sonata is more than twice as long as the first and has four movements rather than one. Prokofiev used sonata-allegro, ternary form, repeated binary form, and sonata-allegro respectively for each movement. In Nestyev's words: "Compared with the first sonata, which is stylistically immature, it presents a great step forward; it is the work of a completely mature personality."[27] Prokofiev used parallel motions and altered chords such as augmented and diminished more frequently than in the previous sonata. Ostinato and polytonality appear noticeably.

The musical texture in this sonata is rich due to sudden contrasts. Prokofiev created contrasts in various dimensions such as between diatonicism and polytonality, between transparency and harmonic density, between extreme dynamic levels, between angular contour and soothing lyricism. The S theme of the first movement in 3/4 meter provides a kind of broad and smooth melody in contrast to the driving P theme. The final movement, initiated with triplet running figures in 6/8 meter, slows down temporarily to let the waltz-like S theme of the first movement join in to generate a reminiscent calmness.

First movement : *Allegro ma non troppo*

This movement contains a driving P theme in triplet motion and a contrasting S theme with broad melody in 3/4 meter. The following diagram shows the overall structural scheme:

Sonata No.2 in D minor Op.14, I : Sonata-allegro (Type III)

STRUCTURE MEASURE NUMBER TONAL SHIFT

Exposition

[26] See Harlow Robinson, *Sergei Prokofiev, a Biography* (New York: VikingPenguin Inc., 1987), 86.

[27] Israel V. Nestyev, *Sergei Prokofiev*, trans. by Florence Jonas (California: Stanford University Press, 1960), 68.

P1	1 – 19	Dm, ***long cadential extension over B***
P1'	20 – 31	Dm
TR	32 – 63	Gm–Gr.$^{+6}$
MC	63	Gr.$^{+6}$–(Em)
S	64 – 85	Em, ***sequences in descending third***
EEC	84 – 85	Em
C	85 – 102	Em, ***parallelism***
Development		
S material	103 – 114	E sustained at melodic part, supported by C_7, ***oblique chromatic motion***
C material	115 – 128	C_7–$G^b{}_7$–***polytonality, Parallelism***
TR material	127 – 158	E^b center–D center,
TR & P cadential material in mm. 10-19	159 – 204	Ends on $G^{\#}$
Recapitulation		
P1	205 – 222	Dm
TR	223 – 254	Am–***parallelism, polytonality, obligue chromatic motion***–Dm
MC	254	A as dominant in Dm
S	255 – 276	Dm over C bass
ESC	275 – 276	A_7–Dm
C	276 – 294	Dm

Coda	295 – 313	Based on P material

The D-minor triad is presented straightforwardly with upbeat A implying dominant that jumps one octave and becomes the fifth degree of the tonic. However, the tonic is destabilized immediately by way of the bass line's descending quasi-chromatic scale. It strongly suggests the appearance of the dominant in m. 8. However, the B and $D^{\#}$ in the lower register in m. 8 make the $C^{\#}$ rather than the $D^{\#}$ in the right hand as an added note (See Ex.2-1).

【Ex. 2-1】Prokofiev Sonata No. 2, 1st movement, mm. 1-8

This seemingly wrongly placed cadential extension refuses to confirm the conventionally expected dominant until the upbeat A in m. 19. In the second appearance of P theme, the actual dominant chord is confirmed in m. 28. A long TR starts in Gm with a repeated i-V alternation that is imitated in ascending parallel motion from Fm、E^{b}m to D^{b}m. The i-V alternation ends in FM in m. 60. The effect of medial caesura is achieved in mm. 63-64 through ascending chromatic motion from A to C in the right hand and from C to $D^{\#}$ in the left hand. Both $D^{\#}$ and F serve as leading tones to E in the S zone after the temporarily stabilized FM in mm. 60-63. The accented C in m. 63 is indirectly resolved to B in m. 64 (See Ex. 2-2).

【Ex. 2-2】Prokofiev Sonata No. 2, 1st movement, mm. 58-68

The S zone is arranged around an E center. The E-minor triad is well established with a preceding passage strongly suggesting a B dominant in m. 84. Measure 85 can be seen as EEC that summarizes the preceding unstable S zone (See Ex. 2-3).

【Ex. 2-3】Prokofiev Sonata No. 2, 1st movement, mm. 79-89

The passage between mm. 85-102 stabilizes Em with some excursions. D minor in the recapitulation is established in a way similar to how the S zone is established in mm. 63-64—this time, with both G# and D# as leading tones to the root and the fifth in D-minor tonic in m. 205 (See Ex. 2-4).

【Ex. 2-4】 Prokofiev Sonata No. 2, 1st movement, mm. 201-206

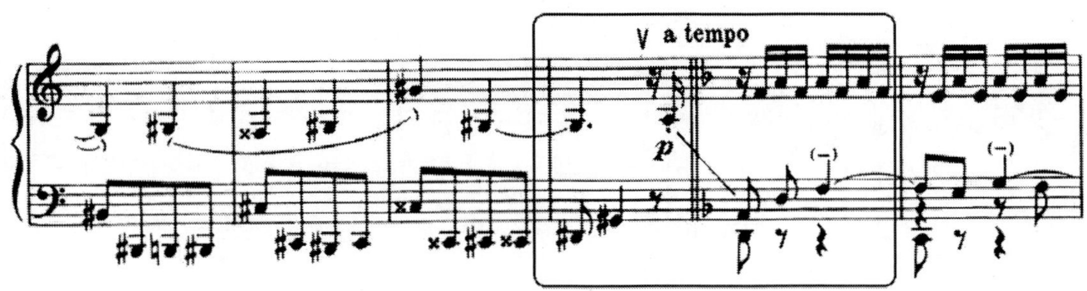

The MC is rather vague in the recapitulation. While S starts in Dm in the right hand, the left hand brings confusion with a C-major triad in m. 255. However, mm. 251-254 show many clues presenting a dominant to Dm; both hands have A and G, the root and the seventh of A_7. In m. 254, the left hand brings out the D tonic; at the same time the D serves as upper leading tone to C in m. 255 (See Ex. 2-5). The MC effect is indeed reached with the rather stable D-minor tonality in m. 254 and the decreasing dynamic to *pp* at the onset of S zone in m. 255.

【Ex. 2-5】 Prokofiev Sonata No. 2, 1st movement, mm. 248-257

Compensating for the unstable S zone, ESC is clearly presented in mm. 275-276 with a strongly suggested V-I progression. Interestingly, Prokofiev delayed the crucial C# in A7 until the region of Dm. C# is now a dissonance in m. 276 (See Ex. 2-6).

【Ex. 2-6】 Prokofiev Sonata No. 1, 1st movement, mm. 272-280

The overall D-minor orientation is sufficiently assured once again in the Coda with a full D-minor triad at the end.

Fourth movement : *Vivace*

The themes in the fourth movement represent Prokofiev's humorous side. Sequential use of melodic fragments, "wrong notes," and repetition of accompaniment patterns are characteristics of this movement in which the S theme from the first movement reappears in the development. Harmonically, the second sonata makes a departure from the first through the extensive use of parallel chords, altered chords, and ostinati. The typical Prokofievian toccata element makes its first emergence with a unison of ostinati in fast tempo. Increased use of short breaks within melodies results in a more succinct quality. The following diagram shows the overall structural scheme:

Sonata No.2 in D minor Op.14, IV : Sonata-allegro (Type III)

STRUCTURE	MEASURE NUMBER	TONAL SHIFT
Introduction	1 – 17	Dm
Exposition		
P	18 – 34	Dm
TR	35 – 50	C_7–A_7–D_7–(B_7)
MC	50 – 51	***BM–(CM)***
Introduction to S	51 – 58	***Features ostinato arround C***
S	59 – 97	CM
S & TR material	98 – 130	***Polytonality***
EEC	131 – 133	CM
Development		
S of first movement	134 – 145	Over C bass
S material	146 – 161	C bass–F bass

P material	162 – 185	G center–C center
Combinations from various Motives	186 – 238	Ends on A_7
<u>Recapitulation</u>		
P	239 – 258	Dm
TR	259 – 274	D_7–B_7–E_7–($C^{\#}_7$)
MC	274 – 275	***$C^{\#}$M – (Dm)***
Introduction to S	275 – 282	Dm
S	283 – 320	Dm
TR & P material over S ostinato	321 – 349	E^b_7–D^b_7–C_7–***side-slipping substitution***
ESC	349 – 350	A_7–Dm
C	350 – 353	Dm

As in the first movement, the D-minor tonality in the fourth movement is clearly stated at the beginning. The introduction is straightforwardly concluded in a V-i progression. The broken D-minor chord remains through the first seven measures in the P zone. A_7 in m. 33 is achieved with an upper neighbor on B^b and lower neighbor on $G^{\#}$ in m. 32 (See Ex. 2-7).

【Ex. 2-7】 Prokofiev Sonata No. 2, 4th movement, mm. 29-37

TR starts with C_7 chord that foreshadow the S zone in C major. The whole passage is shifted whole step higher in mm. 43-50. B-natural and $F^{\#}$ in m. 50 lead to C and G respectively that confirm the MC in m. 51 (See Ex.2-8).

【Ex. 2-8】Prokofiev Sonata No. 2, 4th movement, mm. 43-56

Before the wide-leaping S theme, an eight-measure introduction first establishes the C-major area in mm. 51-58. The S theme appears twice in different registers over an ostinato around the C center. Before EEC comes to confirm the C-major tonality in mm. 131-132, an excursion appears in a polytonal gesture—the left hand stays in C major but the right hand shifts to D major, then to E major in mm. 98-113. EEC is presented with a succinct V-I in C major in mm. 131-132 after a restatement of introductory material from S zone (See Ex. 2-9).

【Ex.2-9】 Prokofiev Sonata No. 2, 4th movement, mm. 121-133

The opening gesture of the development is almost exactly the same as in the development of the first movement. Fragmented S material is combined with the ostinato featured in the S zone. After a long section over C pedal in mm. 134-151, harmonic digression starts with S material with accompaniment focusing on F, which is followed by P material focusing on G in mm. 162-173. Prokofiev often added major or minor seconds to tertian chords in individual ways to give spice to these chords. An example can be found in mm. 160-161.

C dominance returns again in mm. 178-206. Transitional material (not TR in itself) starts from m. 206 that moves from C and eventually comes back to A_7 in the same way as in the opening introduction. The TR in the recapitulation starts from a D-major triad, this time to foreshadow the S zone returning to the tonic key. The MC is stated through the $C^{\#}$ leading tone to D in m. 275, the onset of the S zone (See Ex. 2-10).

TR material (not TR in itself) in m. 321 serves as the basic gesture to distract the expectation of ESC as in the exposition and reaches the ESC eventually in m. 350 with an authentic cadence.

【Ex. 2-10】Prokofiev Sonata No. 2, 4th movement, mm. 270-281

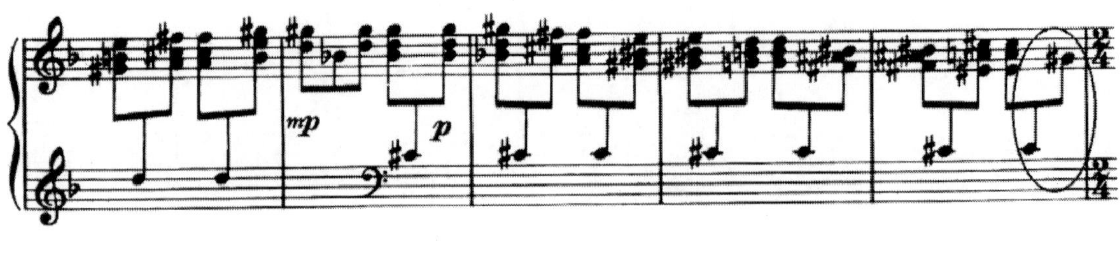

5

Sonata No.3 in A minor, Op.28 (1917)

"When, on October 25, 1917, Lenin and the Bolsheviks seized the Winter Palace, ousted the Provisional Government, declared Russia the world's first socialist state, and ended the short October Revolution, Prokofiev was far away in the Caucasus." [28] Interestingly, 1917 was one of the most productive years in Prokofiev's entire career. It was during these devastating months that he composed several of his most lasting compositions: the *Classical Symphony*, the first violin concerto, *Visions fugitives* for piano, the piano sonatas Nos. 3 and 4, and the cantata *Seven, They Are Seven.* None of these works—with the possible exception of *Seven, They Are Seven* and a few of the *Visions fugitives*—reflects the political and social turmoil that Russia was then facing.[29] Sonata No. 3 forms a pair with No. 4; both bear the subtitle "From Old Notebooks." [30] The notebooks were from Prokofiev's Conservatory years; the mature sonata No. 3 (Op. 28) is a reworking of the third youthful sonata and the mature sonata No. 4 (op. 29) a reworking of the youthful fifth sonata. Despite their similar sources, however, Nos. 3 and 4 are quite different in character. No. 3 is brief—in one movement—and closely follows the youthful version, while No. 4 is more extensive—in three movements—and expansively reworked from its earlier source.[31]

The P theme in No. 3 (*Allegro tempestoso*) is characterized by wide leaps, extended melodic range, and short rests. The S theme represents Prokofiev's lyric expressiveness, which offers a counterbalance to the angular P theme. Harmonically, No. 3 is based on the tertian system; chromatic motion and parallel chords appear frequently. The toccata element is set out in the opening measures. Nestyev states that No. 3 belongs to "Prokofiev the classic, the Prokofiev of imposing sonatas, who knows the secret of impeccable form, who is capable of developing his theme in the grand classical manner

[28] Robinson.
[29] Ibid.
[30] Ibid., 133.
[31] Ibid.

with the convincing power of Beethoven."[32] The following diagram shows the overall structural scheme:

Sonata No.3 in A minor Op.28 : Sonata-allegro (Type III)

STRUCTURE	MEASURE NUMBER	TONAL SHIFT
Introduction	1 – 15	E_7
Exposition		
P1	16 – 26	Am
P2	27 – 43	Am–Em–Bm–C#m
TR	44 – 54	***Over G# bass***
MC	54 – 57	***G#–G7***–(CM)
S	58 – 91	CM
EEC	91 – 93	G_7–CM
Development		
P & S motivic cells	94 – 145	***Chords by oblique chromatic motion, parallelism, superimposed chords***
S as climax	146 – 153	Dm–***Em7***
Recapitulation		
Introduction to P2	154 – 165	E pedal point – Am
P2	165 – 180	E_7–Am
TR	181 – 188	$F^{\#}_7$–E_7
MC	188	E_7–(Am)
S in L.H.	189 – 204	Am

[32] Nestyev, 1946, 68-69.

ESC	204 – 205	E_7–Am
Coda	205 – 334	Am

This sonata bears a long introduction in the region of the dominant in mm. 1-15 that contains essential motivic material for the P theme—the triplet figure and wide leaps. The A-minor effect is clearly brought out after such a long introduction in dominant. The C-major area is stated after a long transitional zone that seems to be leading to C$^{\#}$ minor, by its highlighted G$^{\#}$ bass in mm. 44-53. The placement of MC is implied in m. 54 in the introduction to the S zone. However, it is not fully exposed until mm. 55-57 after shifting to G in the bass and D in the upper voice (See Ex. 3-1).

【Ex. 3-1】 Prokofiev Sonata No. 3, mm. 45-57

The overall S zone is clearly stated in C major and concludes with an apparent EEC in m. 93 through an expanded authentic cadence in mm. 91-93 (See Ex. 3-2).

【Ex. 3-2】 Prokofiev Sonata No. 3, mm. 90-93

Although the recapitulation is somewhat unstable, the iv-V progression leading to the A-minor tonic in the recapitulation is prepared as early as mm. 146-151 in the development through a stressed and prolonged D bass suggesting the pre-dominant chord in A minor. The concluding E_7 is presented in a rather modal sense with G natural in mm. 152-153.

The boundary between development and recapitulation is blurred by way of a long section emphasizing E in mm. 154-164, which is eventually resolved in m. 165 to P2. The MC in mm. 188-189 is connected to a wittily disguised S theme through an ascending chromatic scale leading to E, the initial note of the S theme in A minor in m. 189 (See Ex. 3-3).

【Ex. 3-3】Prokofiev Sonata No. 3, mm. 186-194

A passage in C major in mm. 193-200 provides a temporary digression between S in A minor and the restated A tonic at the onset of the Coda. In this case, the ESC is vaguely presented in mm. 204-205, a V-I progression with dissonance (See Ex. 3-4). However, the movement is powerfully concluded with a prolonged i^{64} in mm. 221-224, which is followed by an unexpected shift to I^{64} in C major in mm. 225-226 and a prolonged E_7 in mm. 227-228 before the clear-cut A minor in m. 229.

【Ex. 3-4】 Prokofiev Sonata No. 3, mm. 204-207

6

Sonata No.4 in C minor, Op.29 (1917)

No. 4 has a character different from the previous three sonatas. All three movements show character other than the passionate romanticism of No. 1, or the toccata lines of No. 2 and No. 3. Right from the opening one notices the lack of the vigor and agitated rhythmic force, suggesting a more restrained and perhaps contemplative nature.[33] In addition to the outer movements in sonata-allegro and sonata-rondo forms, Prokofiev used ternary form in the second movement as in the second movements in all the other multi-movement sonatas.

First movement : *Allegro molto sostenuto*

The P theme begins in a low register and spans over three octaves in range. Although it contains large leaps, Prokofiev managed to avoid any sarcastic impulse, imparting a more serious intent with melodic continuity. The following diagram shows the overall structural scheme:

Sonata No.4 in C minor Op.29, I : Sonata-allegro (Type III)

STRUCTURE	MEASURE NUMBER	TONAL SHIFT
Exposition		
P1 (in aabb form)	1 – 16	Cm
P2	16 – 31	Cm
TR	32 – 39	$B^b{}_7$
MC	39	$B^b{}_7$–(E^bM) ***with side-slipping***
S	40 – 65	E^bM
EEC	64 – 65	$B^b{}_7$–E^bM

[33] Martin, 27.

C	65 – 70	E^bM
<u>Development</u>		
P1 material	71 – 88	***E^bm–sequences***
S & P material	89 – 132	Wandering around Cm –G7
Cadential extension	133 – 137	G7
<u>Recapitulation</u>		
P1	137 – 148	Cm
P2	149 – 158	Cm
TR	159 – 161	Cm–$F^\#$m over $C^\#$ bass
MC	161	$F^\#$m over $C^\#$–(CM)
S	162 – 186	CM–Cm–G7
ESC	186 – 187	G7–Cm
C	187 – 197	Cm, ***chords with added notes***

This movement has very vague medial caesuras both in the exposition and recapitulation. It features prevailing neighbor notes. The very first one appears right before the first chord tone in C minor on the upbeat. The C-minor tonality is well established through repeated ii^7-V-i progressions before P2 appears in a chromatic gesture in m. 17. The MC is suggested in m. 39 through the long leading-tone D that is maintained in the melody of the S theme but resolved indirectly to the E^b bass in m. 40, and F^b as lowered upper leading tone to E^b, with F^b's own upper neighbor note G^b, to an E^b long pedal in the S zone. However, the preparation of a quasi-dominant atmosphere is provided as early as the long B^b bass in m. 32. A clear authentic cadence in mm. 68-69, which reinforce the EEC in mm. 64-65 with chromatic displacement, compensates for the insufficiently presented MC (See Ex. 4-1).

【Ex. 4-1】Prokofiev Sonata No. 4, 1st movement, mm. 66-70

The C-minor tonality is again evidently initiated through a conventional dominant chord that ends the development in m. 136. A brief descending scale achieves the MC with a lowered upper leading tone in m. 161, which should be spelled as D^{b} enharmonically. This time the leading tone in the right hand becomes an integral part of the melody initiating the S theme without being prepared in the previous passage (See Ex. 4-2).

【Ex. 4-2】 Prokofiev Sonata No. 4, 1st movement, mm. 157-167

The S zone in the recapitulation is stably presented over a C pedal. As in the exposition, the ESC in mm. 186-187 does not appear until after a harmonic excursion in mm. 183-184, which is in the same manner as in the exposition. The ESC is colored with added notes (See Ex. 4-3).

【Ex. 4-3】 Prokofiev Sonata No. 4, 1st movement, mm. 183-187

Third movement : *Allegro con brio, ma non leggiere*

The third movement uses recognizable sequence technique, this time with an underlying Alberti-bass pattern. In general, No. 4 follows the tertian system with colorization of added notes and chromaticism. The V-I cadence occurs repeatedly in the P theme and outlines the overall form by appearing at the end of the exposition and recapitulation, both times with added notes obscuring the function. Parallel motion occurs in the S theme and serves as a predominant feature in the main theme of the 3rd movement. The following diagram shows the overall structural scheme: (For the sonata-rondo movements, corresponding parts in rondo form are indicated in brackets.)

Sonata No.4 in C minor Op.29, III : Sonata-rondo (Type IV)

STRUCTURE	MEASURE NUMBER	TONAL SHIFT
Exposition		
P, [A1]	1 – 25	CM, ***neighbor notes***
TR	25 – 39	CM–D, ***sequences in ascending thirds***
MC	40 – 42	D
S, [B]	43 – 66	GM ***with side-slipping***
(EEC)	(59)	
Development		
P, [A2]	67 – 82	CM
(EEC)	81 – 83	(CM)
[C] in aba' form	C (a) 84 – 99 C (b) 100 – 118 C (a') 118 – 133	E^bM ***Harmonic side-slipping*** E^bM–G_7 ***altered***
Recapitulation		
P, [A3]	134 – 153	CM

TR	153 – 177	CM–G_7
MC	177	G_7
S, [B2]	178 – 201	CM, ***quartal chords, neighbor notes***
ESC	201 – 202	***B–C, D#–E***
Coda		
P, [A4]	202 – 213	CM

This movement is in sonata-rondo form, in this case with an unstable S and a rather stable P in the second rotation. Prokofiev used sequences extensively in the TR in mm. 25-39 (See Ex. 4-4).

【Ex. 4-4】 Prokofiev Sonata No. 4, 3rd movement, mm. 23-38

The MC is displayed through a repeated D in mm. 40-42, suggesting the V in G with D and its upper neighbor E^{b}, and dynamic range from *f* to *pp*, while the S them in m. 43 is vaguely presented in G major with frequent side-slippings (See Ex. 4-5).

【Ex. 4-5】 Prokofiev Sonata No. 4, 3rd movement, mm. 39-46

The EEC is vaguely presented in m. 59 as the last chord in G major. In compensating for the unclear EEC, the developmental section starts with a rather stable P theme. The [C] section starting from A^{b} in m. 84 shows Prokofiev's fondness for parallel motion and lyrical trait.

In the recapitulation, the S zone is notably stated after the MC in m. 177, which has a clear V function and is in 3/4 meter. Prokofiev uses quartal chords as melodic doubling to provide dissonant spice in mm. 190-193. In contrast to the first rotation, the ESC in the recapitulation is clearly articulated at the onset of the last-rotation P starting in m. 202, which serves as the coda in the sonata-rondo and the last A section in rondo forms. The whole coda strongly confirms the C-major tonality to the end. The sweeping wide leap introduces P in C major. Albeit with some distracting neighbor notes and side-slippings, the overall P zone is clearly deployed in the traditional V-I progression.

7

Sonata No.5 in C major, Op.38/135 (1923/1953)

Prokofiev spent the summer of 1923 in Ettal[34] with Carolina Codina, who would later become his first wife. The calmness of his Sonata No. 5 (Op. 38), which Prokofiev composed at this time, reflects the serenity of the setting; the emotional directness and lyricism of the sonata perhaps reflects the growing passion of his relationship with Carolina. The first movement *(Allegro tranquillo)* uses only two themes; the P theme in C major is a wonderfully simple and lyrical tune. Although the harmony is chromatic, the piece possesses a refined and intimate classicism, lacking the insolence and dissonant bite that first made Prokofiev's piano music famous.[35] Even the ironic second movement in 3/8 meter has a gentler humor rather than a scornful quality. When Nicolai Miaskovsky, one of Prokofiev's best friends, saw the score, he was amazed by the slow tempo— "Nothing but restraint!"[36] Prokofiev later blamed the sonata's restraint on his weak health: The scarlet fever he had survived in America five years earlier had actually weakened his heart, and he felt less active than usual. Those years in the United States before composing No. 5 had been relatively unsuccessful, except for the well-received Chicago premiere of his opera, *The Love for Three Oranges*, and the Third Piano Concerto. In later years he described his departure from the United States: "I was left with a thousand dollars in my pocket, a bad headache and an overpowering wish to get away to some quiet place where I could work in peace."[37]

Nestyev states that this sonata "shows the composer moving away from the vitality of his early piano compositions toward a cold, formal speculation."[38] Prokofiev worked on the revision of No. 5 in 1953, the year of his death. The 1953 version is commonly known today; my analysis is based on this version.

---

[34] Robinson,177.

[35] Ibid.,178.

[36] Ibid.

[37] Lawrence and Elisabeth Hanson, *Prokofiev, the Prodigal son, an introduction to his life and work in three movements* (London: Cassell and Company, 1964), 116.

[38] Nestyev, 1960, 210.

First movement：*Allegro tranquillo*

The opening theme of the first movement shows Prokofiev at his lyrical best. The melody is both simple and memorable as it quietly unfolds. Ashley points out that "the young intellectual has discovered, acknowledged, welcomed within himself that most elusive of talents, the gift for writing beautiful tunes." [39] Instances of bitonality are more frequent than before. Prokofiev used a favorite device of Stravinsky, bitonality at the interval of the tritone, such as the passage in the development in mm. 82-84.[40] The following diagram shows the overall structural scheme:

Sonata No.5 in C major Op.135, I : Sonata-allegro (Type III)

STRUCTURE	MEASURE NUMBER	TONAL SHIFT
Exposition		
P	1 – 19	CM
TR	20 – 23	CM–Am
MC	23 – 25	***E as dominant in Am***
S	26 – 45	***Am over E bass***
EEC	45 – 46	***Em***–Am
C	46 – 62	Am
Development		
P material	63 – 91	***Quintal harmony, bitonality, P inversion***
TR & S material	91 – 126	***Paralellism, polytonality***
P material	126 – 141	B^{b}M–G_7, ***chords by oblique chromatic motion***
Recapitulation		

[39] Ashley, 171.
[40] Kinsey, 99.

P	141 – 157	CM, ***side-slipping***
TR	158 – 161	***Cm***–CM
MC	161 – 162	G7 ***altered***–(CM)
S	163 – 180	CM, ***parallelism***
Interruption of ESC	180 – 187	C#m–CM, ***side-slipping***
ESC	187 – 188	***B–C, D♭ (C#)–C***
C	188 – 191	CM
<u>Coda</u>		
P material	191 – 202	CM

This movement is in sonata-allegro form. The S zone in A-minor is introduced by MC with iv-i (D-A) and V-i (E-A) in A minor in m. 23-24. However, a passage leading to F in m. 25 is "falsely" resolved to E in m. 26 at the outset of the S zone, which serves as a pedal point that obscures the A-minor tonality implied in the right hand (See Ex. 5-1).

【Ex. 5-1】Prokofiev Sonata No. 5, 1st movement, mm. 21-26

This resolving manner from lowered upper leading tone is frequently used by Prokofiev. TR material initiates the EEC in A minor in mm. 44-45, which resembles the passage before the MC (See Ex. 5-2).

【Ex. 5-2】 Prokofiev Sonata No. 5, 1st movement, mm. 42-45

The A tonic is further verified in the following passage in 6/4 meter from m. 46 that obscures the borderline between the exposition and development. The MC in mm. 161-162 in the recapitulation has lowered upper leading tone D^b as well as leading tone B that lead to C at the onset of the S zone in m. 163 (See Ex. 5-3).

【Ex. 5-3】 Prokofiev Sonata No. 5, 1st movement, mm. 160-165

The C-major tonality is clearly stated over an ostinato centering around C in the S zone in recapitulation. A 6/4-meter interruption in mm. 180-187 appears before the ESC in m. 188. According to the harmonic gesture in mm. 177-179, a C-major triad is strongly expected in m. 180. However, Prokofiev used side-slipping to make an unexpected arrival in C# minor in m. 180. After a four-measure excursion, the expected V-I is finally settled in mm. 183-184.

The succeeding passage largely serves as the corresponding part of the C (*closing zone*) in the exposition. C major is reinforced in the coda from m. 191 that has a metrically augmented P theme and some fragments. Quartal ingredients also appear in this movement on occasion but always within a tertian context, as in m. 16.

Third movement：*Un poco allegretto*

This movement presents a model for a combination of sonata-rondo and type II pattern. As in type II, formal recapitulation with P in the tonic is replaced by a tonal resolution within the S zone. The following diagram shows the overall structural scheme: (For the sonata-rondo movements, corresponding parts in rondo form are indicated in brackets.)

Sonata No.5 in C major Op.135, III : Sonata-rondo

(Mixture of Type II and IV)

STRUCTURE	MEASURE NUMBER	TONAL SHIFT
Exposition		
P, [A1]	1 – 18	CM, ***BM/G#m over C***
TR	19 – 23	***Chromatic motion against C bass***
MC	23	***Introduces F (initial note of S) and C (bass in S)***
S, [B]	24 – 41	***Over C pedal point, Side-slipping***

<u>Development</u>		
P, [A2]	41 – 52	CM
[C]	53 – 79	***Chromaticism***
P bridging material, [A3] ***as in mm.9-10***	80 – 94	***C pedal–E^b pedal***
MC	94	***G_7 altered– C***
<u>Tonal resolution</u>		
S, [B]	95 – 103	CM
ESC	103 – 104	G_7–CM, ***substitution, added notes***
P, [A4]	104 – 115	C center, ***parallelism, added notes***
<u>Coda</u>	116 – 140	CM, ***Parallelism, C pedal***

This movement is in sonata-rondo form combined with Type II features because the third-rotation P, also indicated as [A3], has only the rather unstable P bridging material, a polytonal mixture of B major and C pedal as in mm. 9-10, and connects to key other than the tonic (See Ex. 5-4 and Ex. 5-5).

【Ex. 5-4】Prokofiev Sonata No. 5, 3rd movement, mm. 79-82

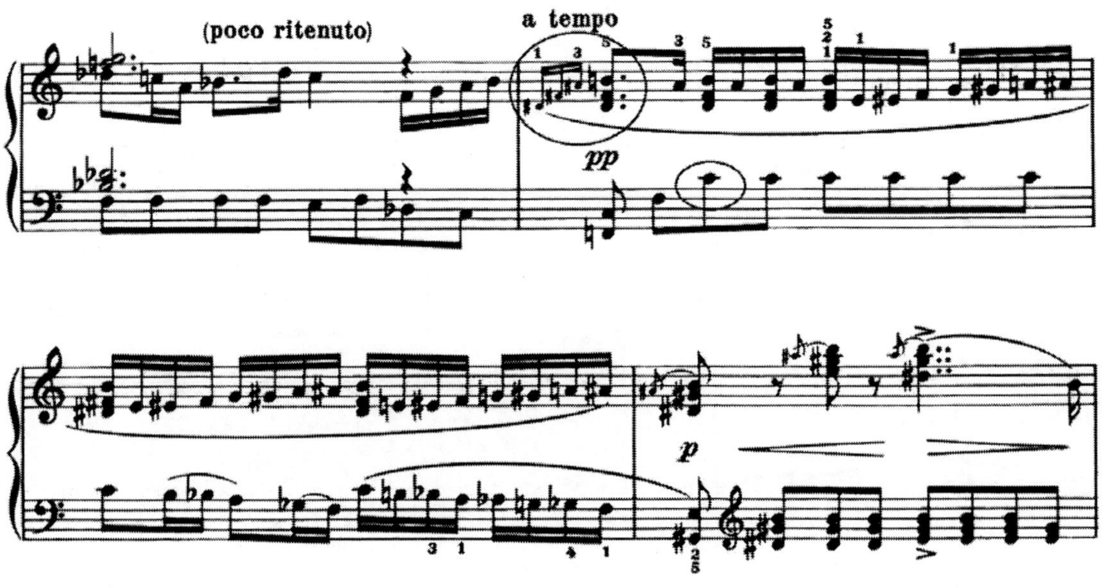

【Ex.5-5】Prokofiev Sonata No. 5, 3rd movement, mm. 7-11

The stable tonic is established at the onset of the S zone in m. 95 (See Ex. 5-6), which also serves as the section of "tonal resolution," a term that substitutes for recapitulation in a Type II sonata.

【Ex.5-6】 Prokofiev Sonata No. 5, 3rd movement, mm. 93-98

P theme in mm. 104-110 is presented in C major over a C pedal with rather dissonant chords between two outer voices that give the impression of transition. The ESC is strongly suggested in m. 104 but undermined right away for its dissonant quality, such as parallel chords with added tritone in mm. 105-109.

The coda wanders around the C center with a stubborn ostinato centered on C. The final chord in the piece is the expected C-major triad.

8

Sonata No.6 in A major, Op.82 (1940)

In several brief articles on life with Prokofiev written by Maria-Cecilia Abramovna Mendelson, often called Mira, Prokofiev's second wife, one of her strongest memories of the summer of 1939 in Kislovodsk was hearing Prokofiev talk about reading Romain Rolland's book on Beethoven, which she claims influenced him in his work on Nos. 6, 7, and 8, all first conceived in Kislovodsk.[41] At the same time that he was writing the extravagantly extroverted paean to Communism, the political cantata *Zdravitsa* (*Hail to Stalin*), Prokofiev began working on his sonatas Nos. 6, 7, and 8 simultaneously during the second half of 1939, after being away from this form for sixteen years.[42] As a piano virtuoso, Prokofiev was keenly aware of the piano's possibilities and its particular musical personalities. Initially, Prokofiev worked on all ten movements of the three sonatas at the same time, switching his attention from one to another as his interest changed. This was not unusual in his working process; he had always tended to think in terms of themes and separate pieces, rarely in entire compositions. That same approach had allowed him to transfer fragments and themes from one work to another so easily—"from *Ivan the Terrible* to *War and Peace*, or from the *Classical* Symphony to *Romeo and Juliet*." No. 6 was completed by the early spring of 1940.

Sonata No. 6 is a gigantic work requiring powerful techniques. In four movements, it represents a return to the highly chromatic and rhythmically eccentric piano music that Prokofiev wrote around the time of the Russian Revolution. The outer movements are respectively in sonata-allegro and sonata-rondo forms. Both second and third movements are constructed in ternary form. The second movement is a whimsical character piece in 2/2 meter featuring extensive use of chords in oblique motion and wide leaps; and the third movement presents another prime example of Prokofiev's lyrical line that is in slow 9/8 meter with thickly harmonized texture. In No. 6, Prokofiev is again the *enfant terrible*, but he managed a masterful combination of optimistic naiveté and insightful maturity.

---

[41] Robinson, 366.

[42] Ibid., 370.

First movement：*Allegro moderato*

The overall gesture of the first movement is filled with biting dissonance and percussive effect, such as chords struck by the fist—*col pugno*. The robustly punctuated opening theme of the first movement is structured around a pounding conflict between A major and parallel A minor. The movement ends on an aggressively dissonant minor second. The central tonality in this movement is challenged by increased dissonance that is manifested through the extremely polyphonic texture and added tones. Imitation at the tritone appears extensively in the development. What is significant in the development is that the themes are used motivically, rhythmically altered, developed contrapuntally, and manifested in various combinations. The following diagram shows the overall structural scheme:

Sonata No.6 in A major Op.82, I : Sonata-allegro (Type III)

STRUCTURE	MEASURE NUMBER	TONAL SHIFT
Exposition		
P	1 – 23	AM
TR	24 – 39	***Chromatic figure–B pedal***
MC	39	G_7 over B
S	40 – 87	CM ***over B pedal***
EEC	87	***A/D over B***
C	87 – 91	***A/D over B***
Development		
S material	92 – 115	***Over B–F, tritone relation***
P material	116 – 128	***Over B pedal***
S & P material	129 – 156	***Over B pedal***

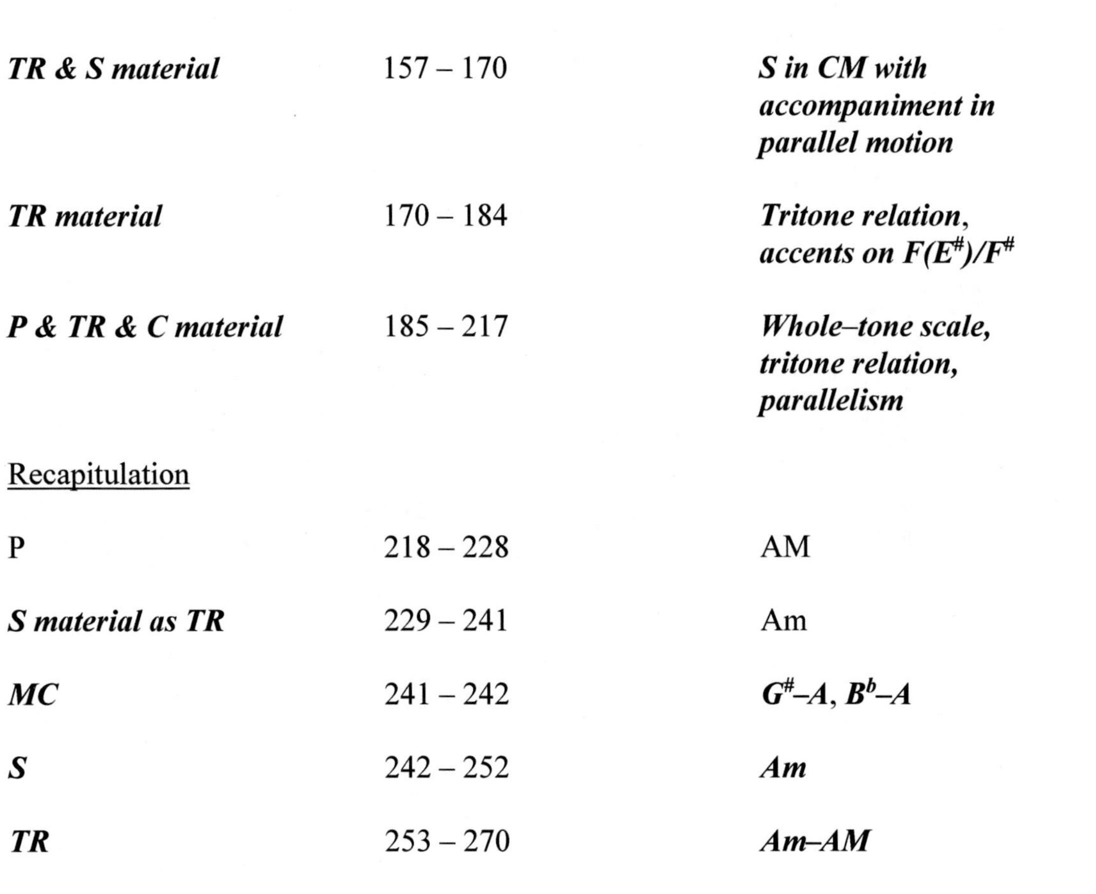

TR & S material	157 – 170	***S in CM with accompaniment in parallel motion***
TR material	170 – 184	***Tritone relation, accents on $F(E^{\#})/F^{\#}$***
P & TR & C material	185 – 217	***Whole–tone scale, tritone relation, parallelism***
<u>Recapitulation</u>		
P	218 – 228	AM
S material as TR	229 – 241	Am
MC	241 – 242	***$G^{\#}$–A, B^{b}–A***
S	242 – 252	***Am***
TR	253 – 270	***Am–AM***
ESC	270 – 272	***AM, P motive, added note***

At the beginning, the alternating A and $D^{\#}$ in the bass initiates the tritone relation that is a crucial element in this movement. After a full A-major triad, Prokofiev used partial side-slipping to provide a tonal clash. On the second beat in the first measure, C and B^{b} substitute for $C^{\#}$ and B in right hand, and $D^{\#}$ occupies the place normally assumed by E in the bass. The P theme is concluded with a V-I progression, which is substituted with $E^{b\,64}$ in the left hand in m. 4. The succeeding cadential extension ends in the same manner (See Ex. 6-1).

【Ex. 6-1】Prokofiev Sonata No. 6, 1st movement, mm. 1-8

After a transition filled with twisting chromatic figures, the MC in m. 39 provides a clear dominant with its root on G and third on B leading to C-major at the onset of the S zone in this key (See Ex. 6-2). The tonality tends to wander between C major and A minor thereafter.

【Ex. 6-2】 Prokofiev Sonata No. 6, 1st movement, mm. 35-45

However, the B bass from previous measures remains through the first three measures 40-42 in the S zone. The same situation is found when the S theme appears for the second time in mm. 52-54 (See Ex. 6-3).

【Ex. 6-3】 Prokofiev Sonata No. 6, 1st movement, mm. 51-55

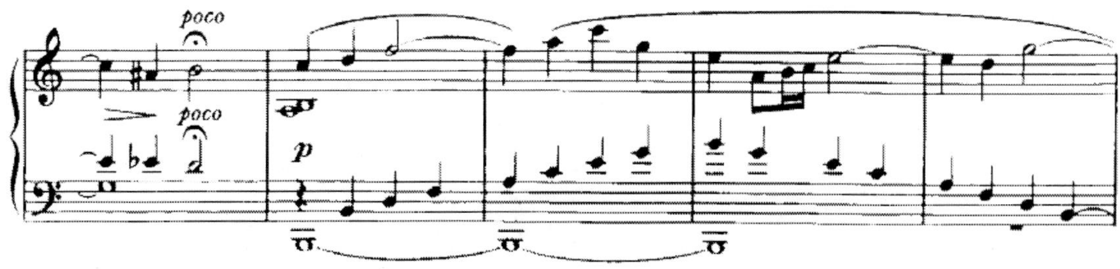

A S-based passage in mm. 64-69 distracts the tonality prior to the transitional passage. It comes back within the region of A minor after m. 86 with a mixing tonal effect of C major and A minor that is extended through m. 91 (See Ex. 6-4).

【Ex. 6-4】Prokofiev Sonata No. 6, 1st movement, mm. 85-91

In the development, Prokofiev used various ways to manipulate motivic cells derived from the P theme and the S theme. The opening three notes of S and the descending third of P are transposed and augmented throughout the development. Contrapuntal devices such as imitation at the tritone are embedded all over (See Ex. 6-5).

【Ex. 6-5】Prokofiev Sonata No. 6, 1st movement, mm. 92-99

The return of A major in the recapitulation is prepared through E7 in mm. 206-217, which is destabilized by B^b and F. These two side-slipped notes serve respectively as upper neighbor to A and E (See Ex. 6-6).

【Ex. 6-6】 Prokofiev Sonata No. 6, 1st movement, mm. 204-212

In the recapitulation, S material starting from A minor in m. 229 is merged with TR material. The MC effect can be noticed through its sudden modal change in mm. 241-242, with lowered upper leading tone on B^b and the leading tone on $G^\#$, both lead toward A. The S zone in A minor, the parallel minor, is undermined by a long descending passage with parallel motion in the left hand in intervals from a third to a sixth in mm. 246-252. Quartal/quintal chords in the left hand provide the tonal clash in mm. 253-260 with descending parallel motion. A large portion of the recapitulation is in A minor. The ESC is not established until the last two measures that confirm the A-major tonality after the long excursion.

Fourth movement : *Vivace*

The final movement, *Vivace*, starts as a witty mixture of Prokofiev's grotesque line and toccata display. This movement is constructed in sonata-rondo form with Type II features that the tonal resolution is not fulfilled until S in the recapitulation. The opening broken triads provide an obsessive background character. Nevertheless, he took an unexpectedly serious turn in the middle, bringing back P theme of the first movement and reinterpreting the same melodic contour in a somber mood. "Masterfully interwoven among the lightly ironic sixteenth-note runs, it produces an eerie and ominous play of light and dark, a sort of *danse macabre*."[43] The following diagram shows the overall structural scheme: (For the sonata-rondo movements, corresponding parts in rondo form are indicated in brackets.)

Sonata No.6 in A major Op.82, IV : Sonata-rondo

(Mixture of Type II and IV)

STRUCTURE	MEASURE NUMBER	TONAL SHIFT
Exposition		
P, [A1]	1 – 16	Am
TR	17 – 27	***Chromatic motion–E–G*****$^{\#}$*****m–CM***
MC1	27 – 28	CM
S1, [B1]	29 – 84	CM
P, [A2]	85 – 99	***B*****^{b}*****m–Am***
MC2	99	***E pedal***
S2 over E, [C1]	100 – 114	***E pedal***
P as TR, [A as TR]	115 – 126	Am
MC3	124 – 126	***Bbm–Am–G*****$^{\#}$*****m***
S3, [D1]	127 – 157	***G*****$^{\#}$*****m***
EEC	157 – 158	***Goes to Am rather than G*****$^{\#}$*****m***

[43] Ibid., 376.

Development

P, [A3]	158 – 184	Am
P motive from first mvt., [E]	185 – 228	Am/AM, ***chromatic scale, Parallelism***
P, [A4]	229 – 289	***$F^{\#}$m–parallelism, Inversion–B^{0}***
MC	288 – 289	***B^{07}implied***

Tonal resolusion

S3, [D2]	289 – 303	Am
S2, [C2]	304 – 317	Am over C
TR	318 – 340	Am–E, ***added note***,
S1, [B2]	341 – 369	AM–***FM***
ESC	369 – 370	Am

Coda

P, [A5]	370 – 430	Am–AM

Repeated V-I progressions confirm the P theme in the A-minor tonic through the first P zone. S1 starting in m. 29 is in C major as in a traditional tonal layout. This movement has a rather expanded S zone that has three themes. The MC is presented in the exposition as a complete C-major triad in mm. 27-28 that leads to S1 in C major in m. 29 (See Ex. 6-7).

【Ex. 6-7】 Prokofiev Sonata No. 6, 4th movement, mm. 26-29

A reminder of P theme in mm. 85-99 is inserted between S1 and S2. A witty design of a third relationship, S2 in mm. 100-115 is presented over E pedal point, namely a major third above C (See Ex. 6-8). Furthermore, S3 starting from m. 126 is centered on G#, a major third above E (See Ex. 6-9). The G# of S3 smoothly shifts to A minor in the third appearance of P in m. 158.

【Ex. 6-8】 Prokofiev Sonata No. 6, 4th movement, mm. 97-106

【Ex. 6-9】 Prokofiev Sonata No. 6, 4th movement, mm. 125-132

A passage suggesting a V-I progression in mm. 156-157 concludes the extensive S zone. This EEC-like passage does not reinforce any tonal center from S themes, but provides a complete natural minor scale in G# that leads to P in A minor. The third appearance of P initiates the development in mm. 158-228. The P zone initiating the development is constantly disturbed by the repeated D# bass, which serves as a lower neighbor to E in a way that suggests the P theme in the first movement. The initial melody in the [E] section as in rondo starting from m. 185 is a reminiscence of the opening P material from the first movement. The tonal resolution is not fulfilled until the S3 in m. 289 after a two-measure MC implied by a B^0 chord.

In reverse order, S2 is stated over C bass from m. 304, then S1 in A major from m. 341. The ascending harmonic minor scale strongly suggests a stable P in A minor in m. 370, which sets off the coda. Nevertheless, the unpredicted F in the bass introduces a long harmonic excursion in the last section. This movement is brought to a close in A major with P fragments from the first movement.

9

Sonata No.7 in B^b major, Op.83 (1942)

No. 7 is smaller than No. 6 in scale and length, with only three movements—*Allegro inquieto* in sonata-allegro form, *Andante caloroso* in ternary form, and *Precipitato* in arch form. Prokofiev gave the key as B^b major, but the first movement has no key signature. Its P and S themes, both notably brief, are highly contrasting: a jockeying and strongly rhythmic phrase in 6/8, and an indolent one in 9/8 meter. Particularly in the P theme, dissonant intervals are prominently, almost grotesquely, displayed, in the manner of "*Suggestion diabolique*."[44] The second movement, lush and warm, introduces a different rhythmic and harmonic world, almost "Schumannesque"[45] in its rich and elaborately accompanied *cantabile* melody. The sonata's concluding movement, *Precipitato*, flourishes with impossibly dissonant chords as well as *forte marcato* between the right and left hand in a "clumsy" but relentless 7/8 meter.[46] The movement is built around a simple, relentlessly repeated and strongly syncopated three-note figure in the bass.

This sonata is a striking epithet of the strength and driving intensity of Prokofiev's (and Russia's) existence during the war years. He entrusted the premier of No. 7 to Sviatoslav Richter, who would first play it—with enormous success—in January 1943 in Moscow. According to Robinson, Richter's premiere was one of the most memorable musical events of the War years:

> *Prokofiev and Mira attended together, in one of their first public appearances in Moscow as a couple. Most of the city's important musical figures were there, too, and when Richter had finished playing, the hall exploded into tumultuous applause. Richter was called back again and again. Prokofiev also appeared on stage to acknowledge the ovation. After most of the audience had filed out, a few musicians who had remained behind, including David Oistrakh, asked Richter to repeat the sonata for them. They wanted to listen more carefully and calmly, savoring its energy and power.*

---

[44] Ibid., 400.
[45] Ibid.
[46] Ibid,. 401.

It was a gratifying moment for Prokofiev, a reward after months of intense and difficult work. [47]

The seventh sonata, winning second place in the Stalin prize competition, was hailed after its Russian premiere as one of Prokofiev's best works.

First movement：*Allegro inquieto*

The first movement is striking in its richness of motivic cells; those of the P theme are used extensively in the development. Contrapuntal devices such as inversion and imitation prevail. The sharp contour and close canonic imitation of the P theme offers a sense of restlessness and urgency. This movement also applies polychords and polytonality as shown in mm. 274-285. The following diagram shows the overall structural scheme:

Sonata No.7 in B^b major Op.83, I : Sonata allegro (Type II)

STRUCTURE	MEASURE NUMBER	TONAL SHIFT
Exposition		
P	1 – 87	***B^b center, B/F tritone relation, P motivic cells***
TR	86 – 118	***B/F center–A***
MC	119 – 123	***A–E^b***
S	124 – 152	***(A)–A^b***
EEC	153 – 154	***Dm^7(tritone from A^b)***
Development		
P motivic cells	155 – 268	***Unusual key relationship***
S & P motives	269 – 289	
TR material	290 – 332	***B pedal***

47 Ibid., 410.

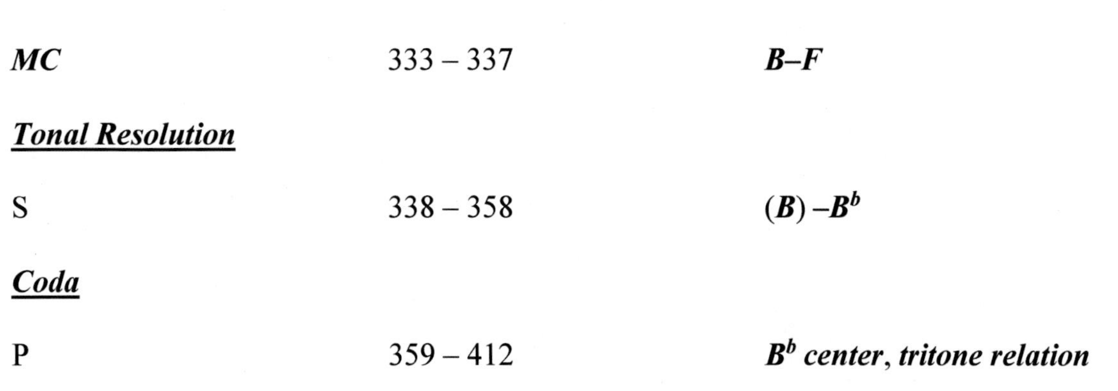

MC	333 – 337	***B–F***
<u>Tonal Resolution</u>		
S	338 – 358	***(B) –B^b***
<u>Coda</u>		
P	359 – 412	***B^b center, tritone relation***
ESC	411 – 412	***First B^{b}M triad***

This movement is the only one not to clearly present the tonic in a functional way. The B^b tonic is surrounded by various neighboring motion (See Ex. 7-1).

【Ex. 7-1】 Prokofiev Sonata No. 7, 1st movement, mm. 1-5

The S zones have a rather noticeable tonal identity due to the open fifths based on the tonal centers on A^b in the exposition (See Ex. 7-2) and B^b in the recapitulation (tonal resolution) between two outer voices.

【Ex. 7- 2】Prokofiev Sonata No. 7, 1st movement, mm. 124-134

This movement provides a good example for the type II pattern due to the fact that its tonal resolution is delayed until the S zone after the second-rotation P. Even the second P is only implied by the transitional figure corresponding to the exposition between P and S. The open fifth established between two outer voices at the beginning of the S zone in m. 338 offers the first place that firmly rests on B^{b} after a long tonal excursion within the return of P material. (See Ex. 7-3)

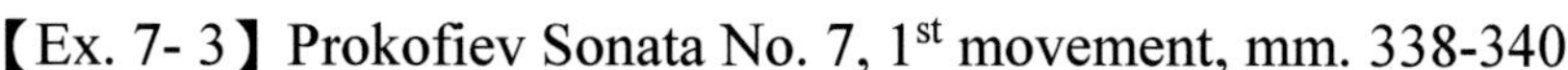

【Ex. 7- 3】Prokofiev Sonata No. 7, 1st movement, mm. 338-340

As in most type II sonatas, the complete statement of the P in the tonic is realized in the coda starting in m. 359 (See Ex. 7-4).

【Ex. 7- 4】Prokofiev Sonata No. 7, 1st movement, mm. 359-364

The opening phrase in the Coda is centering on B^b as at the beginning of the exposition. Instances of polychords and bitonality can be found in mm. 257-285. The ESC is not established until the last two measures with the first complete B^b major triad.

10

Sonata No.8 in B^b major, Op.84 (1944)

No. 8 lacks some of the dissonance and complexity of Nos.6 and 7. It shows increased simplicity and the reflective mood that is a characteristic of No. 9. No. 8 is the last of the three "Kislovodsk" sonatas, all originally conceived during the summer of 1939 in Kislovodsk, when Prokofiev and Mira first met. Dedicated to Mira, No. 8 is both musically and emotionally a gentle and romantic tribute to the love that had helped him survive and create during the difficult years of the War.[48]

Composed in three movements, the predominance of slow tempo in Sonata No. 8 is striking: both the first movement *(Andante dolce)* and the second (*Andante sognando*) are slow, followed by a concluding *Vivace.* "Sweet" and "dreamy" are words rarely associated with Prokofiev or his music, but they occur with surprisingly frequency in No. 8.[49]

Both main themes of the extended first movement are in long, flowing lines. The first is a wandering, thickly harmonized and soft "Schubertian" theme, contrasting in texture with the shorter and more transparent second theme, which, announced in a high register, is fragile and brittle, like a tune from a music box.[50] The second movement is in ternary form in D^b major. The final movement in rondo form features toccata elements in 12/8 meter, with runs primarily in triplets. Throughout the sonata, the intervals of the tritone and second play an important harmonic role, although they are used with somewhat less irony and aggression than in Prokofiev's earlier piano music. After some reservations, Sviatoslav Richter, who knew Prokofiev's sonatas more intimately than any other pianist, considered No. 8 the richest of them all. According to Richter: "It has a difficult inner life with profound contradictions. The sonata is rather difficult to grasp, but difficult because of an abundance of riches—like a tree loaded down with fruit." [51] But Richter did not give the premiere. That honor fell to another brilliant Russian pianist, Emil Gilels, who premiered it in late 1944 in Moscow.

---

[48] Ibid., 430.
[49] Ibid.
[50] Ibid., 431.
[51] Ibid.

First movement：*Andante dolce*

The P theme comprises three distinct themes. The opening material is later modified, resulting in an abca' structure. The following diagram shows the overall structural scheme:

Sonata No.8 in B^b major Op.84, I : Sonata-allegro (Type III)

STRUCTURE	MEASURE NUMBER	TONAL SHIFT
Exposition		
P (in abca' form)	1 – 34	B^{b}M, ***side–slipping***
P1	1 – 9	
P2	10 – 17	
P3	18 – 25	
P1'	26 – 34	
TR	35 – 60	B^{b}M–DM
MC	60	DM
S	61 – 82	Gm–GM
EEC	82 – 89	GM
C	90 – 115	GM
Development		
TR, P material	116 – 168	
S material	169 – 205	
Recapitulation		
P (in abc form)	206 – 231	B^{b}M–E^{b}M
P1	206 – 214	
P2	215 – 222	
P3	223 – 231	
TR	231 – 244	Cm–FM
MC	244	FM–B^{b}m

S1	245 – 260	B^{b}m
C material, ***appear before ESC***	261 – 292	***B^{b}m***
ESC	293 – 297	B^{b}M, ***side–slipping***

The consequent phrase of the opening P theme provides an example of side-slipping. The melody in mm. 3-4 can be revised to D-G-A- B^b- E^b- B^b-F-B-C (See Ex. 8-1).

【Ex. 8-1】 Prokofiev Sonata No. 8, 1st movement, mm. 1-4

The other example appears in m. 12. Prokofiev used C$^\#$-F$^\#$-E to substitute for C-F-E^b in the right hand and F$^\#$-E^b-D^b to substitute for F-D-C in the left hand (See Ex. 8-2).

【Ex. 8-2】Prokofiev Sonata No. 8, 1st movement, mm. 9-15

The bass motion stays relatively firmly within the B^b-major tonality at the beginning. After a long transition, the MC is finally established in m. 60 in D_7 that prepares for the G-minor tonality in the S zone.

The moods between P and S zones are relatively similar in comparison to other sonatas. After confirming the G tonality in its major mode at the EEC in mm. 82-89, Prokofiev provided a contrasting section in the C zone (See Ex. 8-3).

【Ex. 8-3】Prokofiev Sonata No. 8, 1st movement, mm. 80-91

The closing material starting from m. 90 bears a toccata element. Though it follows the tonality in G minor, the right-hand running figure obscures its tonal identity. The P fragment is augmented in bass line in G major mm. 100-107 (See Ex. 8-4).

【Ex. 8-4】 Prokofiev Sonata No. 8, 1st movement, mm. 100-105

The borderline between closing section and development starting in m. 116 is undermined, which is primarily based on TR material (See Ex. 8-5).

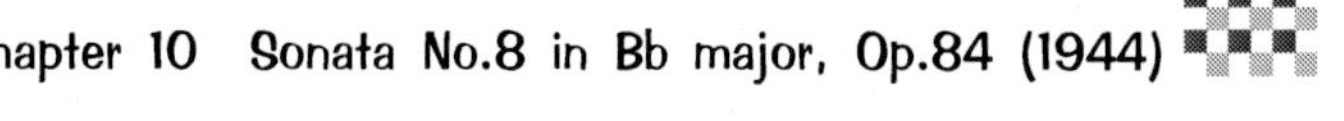

【Ex. 8-5】 Prokofiev Sonata No. 8, 1st movement, mm. 113-118

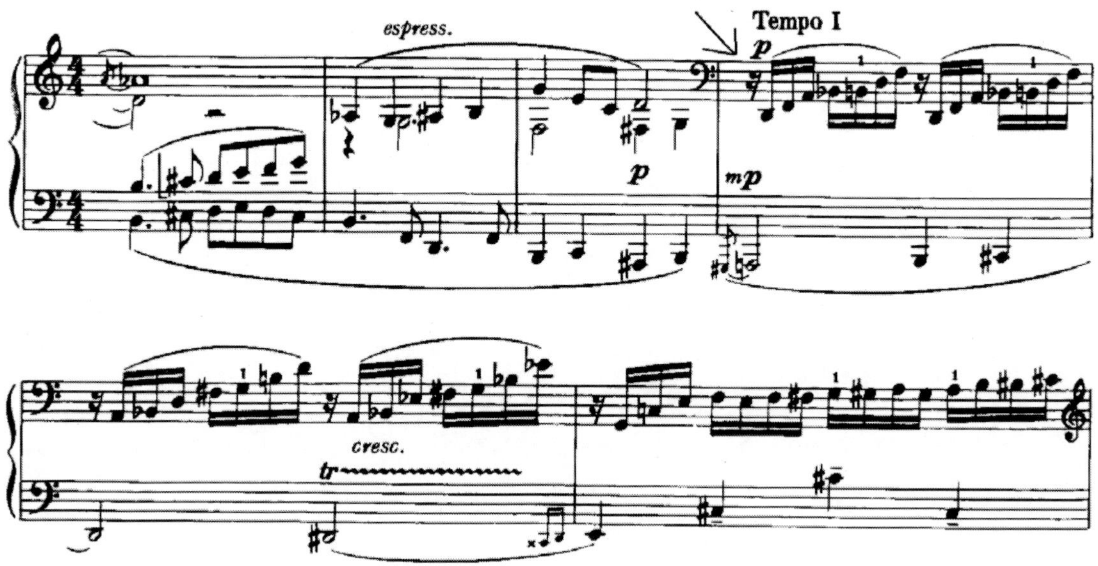

In the recapitulation, Prokofiev used a long section based on C (closing zone) material to delay the ESC, which is achieved in the last measure (See Ex. 8-6).

【Ex. 8-6】 Prokofiev Sonata No. 8, 1st movement, mm. 290-297

11

Sonata No.9 in C major, Op.103 (1947)

Prokofiev dedicated No. 9 to Richter, then the leading interpreter of his piano music. When he first heard No. 9, Richter was surprised—and even disappointed—at its remarkable "simplicity," but he later came to regard it as one of his favorite Prokofiev sonatas.[52] This sonata is "marked by an unaccustomed simplicity, clarity, and above all, serenity."[53] The P theme of the first movement (*Allegretto*), a tranquil theme in 3/2 meter, is particularly diatonic. The S theme, too, is calm and highly lyrical as is the mood of the entire sonata. In the second movement in ternary form, Prokofiev once again used running triplets and dissonant intervals characteristic of most of his fast movements. Nevertheless, an extended slow section subdues the effect. The third movement in rondo form, *Andante tranquillo*, is another example of Prokofiev's reflective side. Filled with dotted rhythms, the fourth movement in sonata-rondo contains one of Prokofiev's trademark marches, "in the style of *Love for Three Oranges*, with quirky open intervals and a clumping bass line."[54] The last movement comes to a tender close with a return to the first movement's quiet main theme over trembling seconds in the left hand, creating a misty effect.

Richter used the special occasion to give Prokofiev a birthday present in 1951: the world premiere of No. 9. "It's a bright, simple, even intimate sonata," said Richter. "To me, it even seems like a kind of *sonata-domestica*. The more you hear it, the more you come to love it and yield to its attraction—the more complete it comes to seem. I love it very much."[55]

All four movements contain codas in which the first theme of the succeeding movement is presented. The finale restates the theme of the first movement, resulting in a totally cyclical form.

---

52 Ibid., 459.
53 Claude Samuel, *Prokofiev*, trans. by Miriam John (London: Calder and Boyars, 1971), 149.
54 Robinson., 459.
55 Ibid., 488.

First movement：*Allegretto*

Nestyev has called the ninth sonata Prokofiev's "swan song in this genre."[56] The S theme is similar to the P theme in its folk-like nature, which evokes an image of a Russian dance (mm. 40-49). These themes show an attempt to incorporate Soviet ideology into his musical principles, which encourages folk-like nature and simplicity representative of the people."[57] The following diagram shows the overall structural scheme:

Sonata No.9 in C major Op.103, I : Sonata-allegro (Type III)

STRUCTURE	MEASURE NUMBER	TONAL SHIFT
Exposition		
P	1 – 19	CM
TR	20 – 36	CM–D_7
MC	37 – 40	D_7–GM
S1	40 – 60	GM
S2	61 – 68	GM
EEC	68 – 69	GM
C	69 – 76	GM
Development		
P material	77 – 90	Over G
S material	90 – 110	
TR material	111 – 119	
P material	120 – 133	Over C

[56] Nestyev, 1960, 395.
[57] Martin, 66.

Recapitulation

P	133 – 143	***Clear restatement but in BM***
TR	144 – 161	BM–CM
MC	161 – 162	G_7–CM
S1	162 – 175	CM
S2	176 – 183	CM
ESC	183 – 184	CM
C	184 – 188	CM
Coda		
P of second movement	188 – 199	CM

As shown in the analytical diagram, the tonal design of this movement is clear-cut. The P theme is stated straightforwardly in C major. The MC over a G bass suggests that the tonal center of the S zone is prepared with repeated $C^{\#}$-D-G in the bass from m. 37 (See Ex. 9-1).

【Ex. 9-1】 Prokofiev Sonata No. 9, 1st movement, mm. 33-41

The brief EEC concluding the S zone with a G-major triad in m. 69 is introduced by G^{b}, which can be spelled as $F^{\#}$ enharmonically, and A^{b} in m. 68 (See Ex. 9-2).

【Ex. 9-2】 Prokofiev Sonata No. 9, 1st movement, mm. 67-70

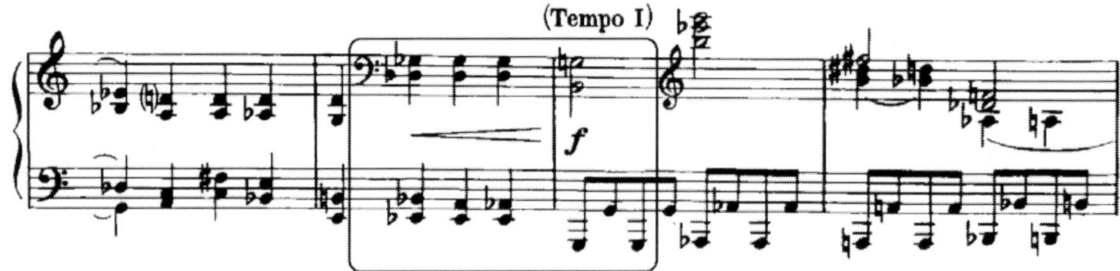

The changing meter distinguishes the development while the character is maintained for the most part. The C pedal in the last section of the development foreshadows the return of C major in mm. 125-132 (See Ex. 9-3).

【Ex. 9-3】Prokofiev Sonata No. 9, 1st movement, mm. 128-136

In balance to the rather stable conclusion of the development in C major, the recapitulated P theme in m. 133 is a half step lower in B major (See Ex. 9-3). The unexpected "wrong" key of B major is colored with side-slipping and parallel motion (See Ex. 9-4).

【Ex. 9-4】Prokofiev Sonata No. 9, 1st movement, mm. 133-143

After the MC with a bass motion suggesting ii-V in C major in mm. 161-162, the S theme is stated mostly over a C pedal. The ESC is stated in mm. 183-184 in the same way as the EEC in mm. 68-69 in exposition. This movement concludes with a passage derived from the second movement.

Fourth movement：*Allegro con brio, ma non troppo presto*

Sequential figures, ostinati, instances of parallel motion, occasional melodic doubling, and conventional triads are applied extensively in this movement. The following diagram shows the overall structural scheme: (For the sonata-rondo movements, corresponding parts in rondo form are indicated in brackets.)

Sonata No.9 in C major Op.103, IV : Sonata-rondo (Type IV)

STRUCTURE	MEASURE NUMBER	TONAL SHIFT
Exposition		
P, [A1]	1 – 9	CM
TR	10 – 23	Am–D_7
MC	24 – 25	D_7
S, [B1]	25 – 39	GM
EEC	39 – 40	***G_7–CM***
Development		
P, [A2]	40 – 49	CM
[C]	50 – 75	EbM
TR based on S material	76 – 87	EbM–G_7
Recapitulation		
P, [A3]	88 – 94	CM
TR	95 – 100	CM–G_7
MC	101 –104	G_7
S, [B2]	104 – 127	CM
P from the 1st movement	127 – 146	CM
ESC	146	***1st complete CM triad***

Like the first movement, the final one also bears a rather noticeable formal structure and tonal design. After the TR begins in A minor, the G-major tonality of the S zone is prepared by the MC through a passage over a D pedal in mm. 24-25 (See Ex. 9-5).

Between the TR and the fragmented scale leading to the MC, parallelism offers a brief harmonic digression in mm. 18-22 (See Ex. 9-5).

【Ex. 9-5】 Prokofiev Sonata No. 9, 4th movement, mm. 16-28

The succinct restatement of P theme in m. 40 starts the development that is overlapped with the placement of the EEC, which is established in C major instead of G major. The developmental quality is illustrated by way of various combinations of motivic cells and sequential arrangements.

In the recapitulation starting in m. 88, the return of C major in the S zone is prepared with the MC in mm. 101-104 in the same way as in the exposition in mm. 24-25 (See Ex. 9-6 and Ex. 9-5).

【Ex. 9-6】 Prokofiev Sonata No. 9, 4th movement, mm. 99-106

However, the C tonality is interrupted with extensive parallel motion. The section in mm. 127-146 confirms the tonic through a complete statement of the P theme from the first movement in the upper voice over continuous turns centering around the C-major scale with some chromatic neighbors. The ESC is delayed until the last measure where we get a complete C-major triad, although colored with a dissonant F#.

Conclusion

The nine sonatas provide a general idea of Prokofiev's stylistic development, which encompasses the romantic trend in his early stage, the establishment of his innovative musical language, and the reflection of his later years as a Soviet citizen. All movements from the nine sonatas are cast in traditional forms. Sonata No. 1 presents the closest example to convention, which demonstrates noticeable structural points with harmonic gestures strongly suggesting the expected arrivals. Frequent use of chromatically altered chords suggests the romantic inclination. Compared with No. 1, No. 2 is a mature example of Prokofiev's personal innovations. Parallel motions, altered chords such as augmented and diminished, ostinati and polytonality appear frequently. The last movement of No. 2 provides a prime model of Prokofiev's toccata line. Sonata No. 3 forms a pair with No. 4; both bear the subtitle "From Old Notebooks". Despite their similar resource, Nos. 3 and 4 are quite different in character. No. 3 features wide leaps and extended melodic range. The S theme provides a contrasting lyrical expressiveness. Chromatic motion and parallel chords emerge frequently without undermining the tertian system. No. 4 has a character distinct from the preceding three sonatas. A restrained and contemplative nature takes the place of the vigorous quality for the most part. The final movement of No. 4 contains more sequential patterns. Chromaticism and added notes enrich the harmonic color. An intimate quality, rarely connected to Prokofiev's music, is the hallmark of No. 5. Another sonata in C major, No. 9, also shares the exceptional calmness and lyrical simplicity. In the first movement of No. 5, instances of bitonality are more common than before.

Prokofiev began working on Nos. 6, 7, and 8 simultaneously in 1939 after he returned to Russia, and these sonatas bear characters that respond to the turbulent wartime and stimulated patriotism. In No. 6, Prokofiev returns to being the *enfant terrible* that he was in Sonata No. 3. It represents the highly chromatic and rhythmically eccentric quality. The first movement is filled with biting dissonances and percussive effect, such as *col pugno.* The central tonality is constantly challenged by dissonance through the utterly polyphonic texture and added notes. The final movement starts as a witty combination of grotesque nature and toccata character. The P theme in the first movement is brought back in the final movement. The same approach was applied in No. 2, but the reminiscence of P in No. 6 bears a rather somber mood compared to the original P theme in the first movement. Though titled in B^b major, No. 7 has no key signature in the first movement. Dissonant intervals are prominent. Sharp contour and wide-ranging contrapuntal devices thoroughly manifest the richness of motivic cells. Although the first movement of No. 7 departs further from a conventional harmonic design, these structural punctuations never fail to find their place in the generative process. In contrast to No. 7, No. 8 lacks some of the dissonance and complexity. It shows increased simplicity and a reflective mood characteristic of No. 9. This work shows Prokofiev's intention to incorporate folk-like simplicity into his music. The tonal design of the first movement is fairly straightforward. The whole of No. 9 is cast in a totally cyclical design; all four movements contain codas in which the first theme of the succeeding movement is presented. The final movement restates the theme of the first movement.

With the analytical concepts derived from Hepokoski and Darcy's sonata-form theory, all structural points are presented clearly or implied with modified treatments. The first movements of all sonatas and the final movement of No. 2 are in sonata-allegro form, type III, except No. 7, which exhibits type II features due to the fact that its tonal resolution is delayed until the S zone, and the preceding P has rather developmental features. All final movements of Nos. 4, 5, 6, and 9 are sonata-rondo, the type IV sonata. Among them, the one of No. 6 is combined with type II features in a less expanded way than No. 7.

The growth of Prokofiev's nine sonatas leads from imitating late romanticism, to increasing complexity, and finally to reflective simplicity. Although disguised with Prokofiev's individual composing manners, the underlying formal structure and tonal deployment are still faithfully rooted in time-honored conventions. The cadential points in Prokofiev's sonatas are clear, despite the fact that "his cadences often finish on unexpected chords or in unexpected keys as the result of abrupt modulations."[58] What seems to be remote from common practice can be understood within functional harmony once we take the chromatic motion, harmonic side-slipping, added notes, and parallelism

[58] Fies, 13.

into account. Prokofiev provided another model for combining convention and modernism, absorbing contemporary idioms as Beethoven did centuries ago in his towering thirty-two piano sonatas.

Bibliography

Ashley, Patricia R. "Prokofiev's Piano Music: Line, Chord, Key." Ph.D. dissertation, Eastman School of Music, 1963.

Blok, Vladimir, ed. *Sergei Prokofiev: Materials, Articles, Interviews.* Moscow: Progress Publishers, 1978.

Burge, David. *Twentieth-Century Piano Music.* New York: Schirmer Books, 1990.

Caplin, William E. *Classical Form: A Theory of Formal Functions for the Instrumental Music of Haydn, Mozart, and Beethoven.* New York: Oxford University Press, 1998.

Chapman Nyaho, William H. "Cyclicism in the War Sonatas of Sergei Prokofiev." D.M.A. thesis, University of Texas at Austin, 1990.

Cadwallader, Allen, and David Gagne. *Analysis of Tonal Music: A Schenkerian Approach.* New York: Oxford University Press, 1998.

Fiess, Stephen C.E. *The Piano Works of Serge Prokofiev.* New Jersey: The Scarecrow Press, Inc., 1994.

Forte, Allen, and Steven Gilbert. *Introduction to Schenkerian Analysis.* New York: W.W. Norton, 1982.

Gillespie, John. *Five Centuries of Keyboard Music.* New York: Dover Publications, Inc., 1965.

Gordon, Stewart. *A History of Keyboard Literature.* New York: Schirmer Books, 1996.

Gutman, David. *The Illustrated Lives of the Great Composers: Prokofiev.* London: Omnibus Press, 1990.

Hanson, Lawrence and Elisabeth. *Prokofiev, the Prodigal Son; an introduction to his life and work in three movements.* London: Cassell and Company, Ltd., 1964.

Hepokoski, James, and Warren Darcy. "Elements of Sonata Theory: The Late-Eighteenth-Century Sonata: Norms, Types, and Deformations." Oberlin College Conservatory and Yale University, 1999. (Later published as "Elements of Sonata Theory" by Oxford University Press, 2006)

Kinsey, David L. " The Piano Sonatas of Serge Prokofiev: a Critical Study of the Elements of Their Style." Ph.D. dissertation, Columbia University, 1959.

Kirby, F. E. *Music for Piano: a short history.* Portland: Amadeus Press, 1995.

Kostka, Stefan. *Materials and Techniques of Twentieth-Century Music.* New Jersey: Prentice Hall, 1990.

Lewin, David. *Musical Form and Transformation: 4 Analytical Essays.* New Haven and London: Yale University Press, 1993.

Martin, Rebecca G. "The Nine Piano Sonatas of Sergei Prokofiev." D.M.A. thesis, University of Kentucky, 1982.

Minturn, Neil. *The Music of Sergei Prokofiev*. New Haven: Yale University Press, 1997.

Morgan, Robert P. *Twentieth-Century Music.* New York: W. W. Norton & Company, 1991.

Nestyev, Israel V. *Prokofiev.* Trans, by Florence Jonas. California: Stanford University Press, 1960.

________. *Prokofiev*. Trans. by Rose Prokofieva. New York: Alfred A. Knopf, 1946.

Newman, William S. *Beethoven on Beethoven, Playing His Piano Music His Way.* New York: W. W. Norton, 1991.

________. *The Sonata Since Beethoven*, 3rd ed. New York: W. W. Norton & Company, 1983.

Prokofieff, Sergei. *Complete Sonatas for the Piano* [Musical score]. Taipei: Chuan Yin Music Publishers, Co.

Prokofiev, Sergei. *Prokofiev by Prokofiev: A Composer's Memoir.* Translated by Guy Daniels. New York: Doubleday & Company, 1979.

Prokofiev, Sergei. *Soviet Diary 1927 and Other Writings.* Translated by Oleg Prokofiev. Boston: Northeastern University Press, 1992.

Roberts, Peter D. *Modernism in Russian Piano Music: Skriabin, Prokofiev, and Their Russian Contemporaries.* Bloomington: Indiana University Press, 1992.

Robinson, Harlow. *Sergei Prokofiev, a Biography.* New York: Viking Penguin Inc., 1987.

________, trans., ed. *Selected Letters of Sergei Prokofiev.* Boston: Northwestern University Press, 1998.

Rolland, Romain. *Romain Rolland's Essays on Music.* Edited by David Ewen. New York: Dover Publications, Inc., 1948.

Rosen, Charles. *Sonata Forms*, rev. ed. New York: W.W. Norton & Company, 1988.

________. *Beethoven's Piano Sonatas: a Short Companion.* New Haven: Yale University Press, 2002.

________. *The Classical Style: Haydn, Mozart, Beethoven*, rev. ed. New York: W.W. Norton & Company, Inc., 1998.

Samuel, Claude. *Prokofiev.* Translated by Miriam John. London: Calder and Boyars, 1971.

Scruton, Roger. *The Aesthetics of Music.* New York: Oxford University Press, 1997.

Seroff, Victor. *Sergei Prokofiev : A Soviet Tragedy.* New York: Funk & Wagnalls, 1968.